ME

DONALD J. TRUMP

YOU CAN'T SPELL
AMERICA WITHOUT
ME

THE REALLY TREMENDOUS INSIDE STORY OF
MY FANTASTIC FIRST YEAR AS PRESIDENT

DONALD J. TRUMP

A SO-CALLED PARODY BY
ALEC BALDWIN & KURT ANDERSEN

★ ★ ★ ★ ★ ★ ★ ★ ★ ★ ★ ★ ★ ★ ★ ★ ★ ★ ★

PENGUIN PRESS 2017 NEW YORK

PHOTOGRAPHY BY MARK SELIGER
© MARK SELIGER

COVER & INTERIOR DESIGN BY EIGHT AND A HALF
CREATIVE DIRECTION BY BONNIE SIEGLER

★

PENGUIN PRESS
AN IMPRINT OF PENGUIN RANDOM HOUSE LLC
375 HUDSON STREET
NEW YORK, NEW YORK 10014
PENGUIN.COM

PHOTOGRAPHS OF IVANKA TRUMP: Michael Loccisano / Getty Images:
page 48 (left) (also on pages 96–97); Peter Kramer / Getty Images: 48
(right) (also on 96–97); Evan Agostini / Getty Images: 86–87 (left); Lars Niki /
Getty Images: 86–87 (right); Dimitrios Kambouris /
Getty Images: 130–131; Lars Niki / Getty Images: 162–163
PHOTOGRAPHS ON BOOK COVERS: Mary Ellen Matthews: 8 and 90
PHOTOGRAPH OF THE WHITE HOUSE: David Everett Strickler / Unsplash: 104

ISBN: 9780525521990 (HARDCOVER); 9780525522003 (E-BOOK)

★ ★

PRINTED IN
THE UNITED STATES OF AMERICA

★ ★

1 3 5 7 9 10 8 6 4 2

SET IN TIMES ROMAN, PERPETUA, AND COMPACTA

TTT

*For my fellow Americans,
who deserve only the best,
and now finally have it –
the richest, smartest
&
most amazing president ever*

TTTTTTTTTTTTTTTTTTTTTTTTTTTTTTTTTTTTTTTTTTTTT

★ ★ ★ ★ ★ ★ ★ ★ ★ ★

MY TABLE OF CONTENTS

★ ★ ★ ★ ★ ★ ★ ★ ★

★ ★ ★ ★ ★ ★ ★ ★ ★

YOU ACTUALLY CAN'T SPELL AMERICA WITHOUT "ME"

I remember the day this all began, the "journey to the presidency," as my daughter Ivanka calls it. It was a really, really fantastic day, one of the best days of my entire life. I've had so many great days—the day my mom finally made my father stop calling me "the Grouchy Little Homo," the day my net worth got bigger than his, the day of my first *60 Minutes* appearance (before CBS News was fake news), the day *The Apprentice* got 28.1 million viewers, the days each of my five children were born, including Tiffany. So many phenomenal, incredible days.

It was in January 1986, the day the space shuttle blew up, so tragic, but I was in a fabulous mood. My first casino in Atlantic City was doing unbelievably great, making so much money, and I'd just made a great deal to take it over and make it more successful by renaming it Trump Plaza. I was in my thirties, and I'd just met one of my future wives, Marla Maples, who was twenty-one, maybe twenty-two, and at that time a nine-plus in the looks department, to be perfectly frank. I was in Palm Beach, my wife

Ivana was doing her thing, and I drove my Rolls-Royce over to The Breakers hotel to visit the legendary genius Roy Cohn, my extremely tough lawyer and personal friend. Roy kept a suite at The Breakers, which had recently refused to let me buy two penthouses and combine them, the morons, because they'd now be so valuable as historic residences. In the dozen years I'd known Roy, he had taught me about the importance of maintaining a strong, great suntan all year long, but I remember that day he was very pale, I guess he was sick by then, AIDS, sad, so I decided to cheer him up by driving him down to Mar-a-Lago for a tour of the place.

I'd just closed on Mar-a-Lago—it was such an amazing deal, one of the best deals I ever made, not the biggest but one of the most outstanding. I bought it for a fraction of what I'd offered only a few months earlier, because I told the owners I'd acquired the whole beach directly behind the house and could totally block their view with a new building, which basically meant selling to me or nobody. (That wasn't completely true, but they were weak and scared—to be perfectly honest, like so many people born into money who aren't Trumps, and even some who are.) And one of the sellers, the B-list snob actress Dina Merrill, was such an un-believable un-PC-word to me. In fact, by the way, since they were technically a foundation, letting me take them to the cleaners, even though I hadn't actually closed on the beachfront lot, people told me it was probably some kind of fiduciary crime on their part.

Anyway, there I was with Roy Cohn, who respected me greatly, at Mar-a-Lago, the most beautiful, amazing, prestigious home in Florida, one of the most beautiful and prestigious in the United States or the entire Western Hemisphere, probably in the whole world. Which I now owned, for almost nothing. It was totally empty, except for the Hispanics and the African Americans— great people scrubbing off the mold and hatcheting the lizards and so forth.

"My Xanadu, right?" I said. Roy understood I meant William Randolph Hearst's house in my favorite movie, *Citizen Kane*, because like me, Roy was very smart, Ivy League but not a phony. He mentioned that Marjorie Merriweather Post, the Shredded Wheat and Honey Bunches of Oats heiress who built Mar-a-Lago, had meant it to be used by American presidents as a Winter White House. Most presidents, then just like now, couldn't afford extremely nice homes of their own, not even to rent.

★ ★

"YOU KNOW WHAT, ROY?" I said. We were standing on one of the beautiful marble verandas—it's covered in fifteenth-century Spanish tiles, that's the *1400s*, when Spain and those people were on top, each tile now worth $25,000, half a million pesos apiece—and I was looking out at the ocean, not in a sad way, but more kind of a wise way. "It's really a shame that Donald Trump can't ever be president," I said. "Not that I'd necessarily want to be. My life is better than a president's in a lot of ways, much better. In most ways. Did you know Reagan only makes two hundred grand a year? But what I hate is that because of that one *law* I *can't* be president, only because of that stupid, ridiculous law."

Roy was rubbing one of the carved stone griffins, the weird little gay royal dragon things all around Mar-a-Lago. "What 'law'? You mean the problem with that punk in Atlantic City? Don't worry about him. Forget him. He's gone. He doesn't exist. Literally."

"No, no," I said, "because of my mom. Because she's from Scotland."

Roy explained that all these years I'd had it wrong—a foreign *parent* doesn't mean you can't become president. Article something, clause whatever.

"*Wow*," I said. "Wow. And in a few months I turn forty. You know what *that* means."

"You're dumping Ivana? Fine. Don't tell her until after we get the new postnup drafted and signed."

"No, it means I'll be old enough to run for president! Nothing stopping me! Mar-a-Lago could actually be *my* Winter White House someday, Roy!"

"You can be elected president *now*, Don. The minimum age is thirty-five, not forty. Same article, same clause." Even with the AIDS, Roy had a very brilliant legal mind.

At that moment, I saw a whole new direction my life could go, all kinds of new angles I could play. Roy died a few months later, but people have told me he actually died much happier after he knew he had cleared the way for my greatest deal and greatest achievement of all—that he was my mentor, and I was his John F. Kennedy, if Joseph Kennedy had been gay and Jewish and his son had been Protestant. Proud that someday I would, you know, make America great again. But also so I could prove once and for all, beyond any shadow of a doubt, that Trump is an important man the world should never ignore or laugh at. A great American winner at business? Sure. A sexy guy who attracted a thousand beautiful ladies, supermodels and entertainers and many others? Definitely. More importantly, a highly intelligent and strongly trustworthy leader who people really, really, really admire, who millions and eventually billions of people would really, really, really love and respect forever.

HE WAS MY MENTOR, AND I WAS HIS JOHN F. KENNEDY, IF JOSEPH KENNEDY HAD BEEN GAY AND JEWISH AND HIS SON HAD BEEN PROTESTANT.

That was the day, almost thirty-two years ago, when my brand was just beginning to become a very hot brand, long before it was the hottest brand in the world, I realized that you actually can't spell America without *me*. Literally. Which is so amazing when you think about it.

★ ★ ★ ★ ★ ★ ★ ★

I HAD TO DO IT MY WAY

T he chapter you just read was written personally by me, Donald Trump. I swear it, on the life of my youngest daughter. What you're reading now, I am also personally writing. This entire book: me, all the words and sentences and larger sections, the paragraphs, the chapters, all mine, not "as told to" or "with" some pathetic low-life parasite ghostwriter.

This Trump book, unlike my many previous excellent Trump books, which were typed up by subcontractors who interviewed me, is being created 100 percent by me. It will be, if I can be completely honest, the best one. It already is.

There are many reasons I'm writing it myself. But the basic problem is trust. Who can we totally trust? *Family*. And by that I mean children—and maybe grandchildren, too, my oldest is ten, so I can't say for sure—but not wives or adopted children because, sorry, they don't contain your genes. Although I've heard you can inject people with your genes and make them related to you by blood, which is interesting. Genes, someone once told me, probably Dr. John Trump, my brilliant uncle at MIT, are like computer chips that give you a kind of Bluetooth connection mentally to your children, a kind of remote control over them. It's how you own your children and grandchildren the way you own your homes, which is comforting, and why you love them.

But back to trust. I trusted the third-rate clown who "wrote" my phenomenally best-selling first autobiography, *The Art of the Deal*, and gave him many millions of dollars—but then thirty years later, because nobody had ever heard of him since, as soon as I ran for president he betrayed me. "He's a *Judas*," a lot of my Christian supporters said, which was true, and I like hitting back, but "Judas" seemed a little rough. Some of my supporters say that a lot about the people who hit me— even about people like John McCain, who's Protestant, and Paul Ryan, who's Catholic—and I always wonder if that makes my son-in-law Jared Kushner feel bad, or even Ivanka, who's now technically one also. I'd asked Steve Bannon, my campaign CEO and first White House chief strategist, if he would arrange to have them turn down the "Judas" stuff a little. Not good.

WHO CAN WE TOTALLY TRUST? *FAMILY.* AND BY THAT I MEAN CHILDREN—AND MAYBE GRANDCHILDREN, TOO, MY OLDEST IS TEN, SO I CAN'T SAY FOR SURE—BUT NOT WIVES OR ADOPTED CHILDREN BECAUSE, SORRY, THEY DON'T CONTAIN YOUR GENES.

Then I trusted a nice lady at The Trump Organization, former ballerina, used to be gorgeous, who helped write a few of my recent bestsellers—including *Trump: How to Get Rich*, *Money Does Buy Happiness*, *The Amazing Magical Miraculous Mr. Trump*, and *Everyone But You Is a Loser*. So I let her write my wife's little speech for the Republican convention. By using

Michelle Obama's convention speech for that, she didn't betray me on purpose—my top security guy, Keith, spent a few hours alone with her making sure, believe me—but she did give the dishonest hater disgusting fake media an opportunity to embarrass me and, sure, my wife, on the day of my nomination. Although as Ted Nugent said to me when that blew up, he goes onstage at every concert and plays songs by Chuck Berry and Sam & Dave and the Temptations and Jimi Hendrix and so on, and everybody thinks that's totally okay.

Some earlier Trump books, all huge bestsellers even though "I" didn't "write" them.

Since this will be my greatest and most important book yet, there was another problem: What "professional writer" could I trust to understand and truly *love* Trump? Sean Hannity volunteered to write it, and I believe Sean does love me with the kind of total loyalty I rarely see in high-net-worth individuals who aren't related to me. But I'm sure that like almost all successful people, Sean hires ghostwriters to write his books. Plus, with his show to do every night, which is extremely important for our country, he wouldn't be able to do what I needed—be around me all the time, in every meeting, seeing and hearing it all, taking notes. *Then* the lawyers told me that any outside writer would have to get the top, top, top security clearance, too, which would make the lying, fake media go crazy—although, about that, Bannon said "a feature, not a bug," which is true and funny, but Ivanka convinced me it wasn't worth the fight.

Everybody thought they'd convinced me to drop the idea of doing this book. Can't be done. Too hard. Too many other things on my plate, all the making-America-great things. Even though they also all agreed I have been making America great in so many ways for years, quietly, sometimes anonymously.

"Wait until you're out of office, Daddy," Ivanka said, "when you can say *everything* you want to about Ryan and Merkel and the Clintons and everybody else, and you'll get paid even more."

"That's *Mr. President-elect* Daddy to you," I replied, with a little pinch, as usual, "but do the math, baby. After eight years, I'll be almost eighty. I know you say 'eighty is the new forty,' but I don't want to wait that long to bring out the true story." And I probably won't want to stay in office any longer than that, although as Jared said, Mike Bloomberg got the system in New York fixed so he could stay mayor for an extra four years. And a friend told us that a friend of his in Europe, the president of Belarus, which is an actual European country, did the same thing, so he's been the elected president there for twenty-two years and counting. So anything's possible. And Trump specializes in doing the impossible. And then I'd be the first U.S. president in like a century, since FDR, to go more than two terms. That would be very special.

If you tell Trump he can't do something, that makes him do it. Like my MIT uncle Dr. John Trump, PhD, taught me, "Every action causes a much, much bigger reaction against it." The other great thing about me is that if I have a problem with one of my businesses, I always step in and fix it myself. (For instance, that's what Roy Cohn was referring to in the previous chapter, concerning the dishonest person causing the problem when I was building my casinos in Atlantic City.)

So for this book, I decided I really had to do it myself. I had to do it *my way*.

Incidentally, that's my favorite song, "My Way." I love my Native American friend Wayne Newton's version, which he sings for me every time I see him, almost whispers it in my ear, so fantastic. (Which means I've had the opportunity to examine that very expensive face of his up close. Whoa.) I was going to print the lyrics to "My Way" right here until I found out how they screw you for that, even though you can read them for free on the Internet. Unbelievable! So why would I pay thousands of dollars to the composer, the very overrated Paul Anka, who wouldn't even perform at our great inauguration?

Hold on, before I forget.

> *VOICE MEMO: Presidential to-do list*
> *Write songs, words, not music—have them recorded*
> *by Nugent, Meat Loaf, the Jackie girl from the*
> *inauguration, Kanye et cetera.*

Okay, I'm back. You see, I'm actually saying this book right into my phone. It's amazing. I talk, I create it, it types, *talking is writing* nowadays, which is so great. And the beauty of this is that the computer in my phone doesn't need a security clearance, and it won't put in words I would never use or betray me or quit, like the ghostwriters. I *own* this phone.

My brilliant ten-year-old showed me how to push a button on the screen to make it tape my conversations whenever I want, even when it's in my jacket, and then later turn those recordings into words, too. So you, the reader, will be right here with me, wherever I am as President Donald Trump—in the Oval Office, in the foreign countries I visit, inside the underground command rooms, flying on NASA's secret presidential rocket to inspect our secret bases on the moon, which Alex Jones tells me definitely exist. I'll be reporting my inside story "in real time," as Jared calls it, which I like because that also means it's the opposite of *fake* time. "You could do it in present tense," he said, "which would make it more exciting to readers." Right, I told him, exactly. Because I knew that "present tense" means words that express an action or state in the present moment and

> **I'LL BE REPORTING MY INSIDE STORY "IN REAL TIME," AS JARED CALLS IT, WHICH I LIKE BECAUSE THAT ALSO MEANS IT'S THE OPPOSITE OF *FAKE* TIME.**

are used concerning that which is true at the time of writing or speaking. Examples include: "I am talking into my phone from my amazing apartment at the top of Trump Tower, and the people on the street down below look even smaller than ants, more like ticks or lice," or "It is so fantastic being president-elect of the United States of America."

Writing my president book by talking makes it possible for me to do it, but if I'm being honest, which I always am, the idea of doing the whole book all by myself was at first . . . made me . . . seemed like . . . oh, what is that word the phonies always use? That fake positive word when they don't want to admit they feel scared or stupid—right, okay, dot-dot-dot: Writing a whole book by myself seemed like a serious *challenge*.

I had one of the girls bring me a few of the recent president memoirs, which are unbelievably long. And, I'm sure, if you read them, which probably nobody does in those cases, unbelievably *boring*. My very intelligent youngest son did the arithmetic—Bill

Clinton's book is like four hundred thousand words and even the one by George W. Bush is two hundred thousand. Give me a break! What are they trying to prove? And by the way, it shows those two guys have no business sense whatsoever, because publishers do not pay you a nickel more for writing more. They pay you *per book*, so get ready for the first sequel, probably in 2018, *You Still Can't Spell America Without Me!*

I HAD ONE OF THE GIRLS BRING ME A FEW OF THE RECENT PRESIDENT MEMOIRS, WHICH ARE UNBELIEVABLY LONG.

But I'm not a "professional writer," one of my family members warned me, although at first I thought she was saying "professional *fighter*." Oh, I told her, I guess you're the house expert on what makes somebody a *professional* or not, but I wasn't a professional TV star until I decided to become one of the most successful of all time, was I? I wasn't a professional politician until I decided to become the most successful of all time. But then Barron, who's not just my youngest son but I also think quite frankly my smartest one, told me the secret truth: I've already written more than thirty thousand tweets, and each tweet is twenty-five words, which means like a *million* words in the last few years. So I'm actually a very, very *successful* writer with millions of readers and years of experience. Jared says he has a guy—one of the European guys who did such great Internet work for us during the campaign—who'll make me an "app" that automatically eliminates most of the quotation marks I use to spice up the tweets and turns the exclamation points into periods. I told him okay, but I also want another app that turns any word I say into all capital letters if I want, just by my thinking it. Which I bet the Pentagon has.

We're going to auction this book to all the publishers after I'm finished. Did you realize most of them are foreign-owned now?

Which is very, very interesting. Very. Anyhow, my "floor," as we say in business, is $60 million, because that's what Barack and Michelle Obama are getting for their *two* books. And by the way, this book, my book, the Trump book, is now out *before* theirs, even though Obama was president before me. The First Lady has an approval rating even higher than mine, ridiculously high—this is her honeymoon period, good for her—but frankly I don't think a publisher will pay all that much for a book by her. I'm not saying that just because of the funny English, or because she's not angry like Michelle, with a million opinions about everything. The American people *like* Melania because she's very beautiful and she's with me, but also because she *doesn't say much*, so why would they want to read a book by her? It's a sad "Cash-22." If you don't know it, that's a word Steve Bannon uses, meaning a real-life good news–bad news joke—like, say, a guy who could get literally any woman any time but can't because he's being watched every minute, like he's in prison—that's a Cash-22.

Millions of people are now buying this book—*you* did, right?—for the same reason people voted for me and the same reason that even the haters can't stop reading about me and talking about me and thinking about me and actually dreaming about me. Because I'm not a phony, and I'm totally honest in a way nobody else in this position has ever been.

I promise everything here is 100 percent true, *so* true, all of it. People are already telling me it may be the truest book ever written. It is the unauthorized, uncensored inside story of me *by* me— thanks to technology, from my brain to my mouth to your eyes and ears and brain directly. It's like you and I are making out and I'm just shooting information into you, shooting streams of thought and my true "me" into you. (Although if you're a man, it's like we're merging and sharing power in a sci-fi movie scene, like Obi-Wan Kenobi talking directly to Luke Skywalker from heaven.) I'm going to tell you things they don't want me to say as president, not in the speeches or the press conferences or even on Twitter—and I can do that here because I'm not writing *as* the president, okay, but as Donald Trump, just another American citizen who also happens to be president, so . . . freedom of expression, First Amendment, totally honest, no holds barred, the whole truth, nothing but the truth, all for you and us, the great American people.

THIS IS AMERICAN HISTORY

I woke up at dawn, like always. But where was I?

No monogrammed Ts, not on the sheets, not anywhere!

Then I remembered: It was the 20th of January. Ivanka and Jared convinced me I had to obey "tradition"—meaning the night before my inauguration I couldn't stay in the Trump Townhouse at the Trump International Hotel, which is the biggest hotel suite in Washington and probably in America, 6,300 square feet, with its own entrance on Pennsylvania Avenue and a *six-fixture* master bath including a steam shower. No, I was in Blair House, behind the White House. With my beautiful wife, the First Lady–elect, *I* was in Obama's guesthouse, *behind* the mansion, like in the White House slave quarters. Kind of unbelievable, right?

It was my final morning as Donald Trump, private citizen—yes, unbelievably rich private citizen who built the world's largest and greatest business of its kind, private citizen already more famous than anybody on earth *ever*, according to some professor's analysis. But even so, I knew my life would change forever when I became Donald Trump, President of the United States of America, Commander in Chief of the Armed Forces, and Leader of the Free World, even though they tell me that last one isn't an official title anymore. I felt the way you feel right before you get married the first time—about to stand in front of a big crowd, most of the people don't really know you, old words you have to say, promises you mean when you say them to the minister or judge or whatever. Except becoming president really *is* forever in a way marriage isn't, unless you marry somebody extremely rich or "legacy famous," like Jackie Kennedy Onassis, who by the way wanted to date me in the 1970s, but she was already fifty.

Starting around lunchtime, I would be officially equal to or better than John F. Kennedy, George Washington, Ronald Reagan, Thomas Jefferson, Abe Lincoln, all of the Roosevelts. (By the way, I knew Reagan, consulted with him at the White House. People say he had a sixth sense that I would eventually be one of his successors. Congratulations, President Reagan, you're welcome—even if you already had a touch of the Alzheimer's then, I've now proved you right!) I never really understood what people mean when they say after some big win, a huge score, "Oh, it '*humbles*' me, I feel so '*humbled*.'" Such phonies. I still don't get it, but I guess something like that is what I felt the day of my inauguration. It did feel *big*, very, very big, the biggest ever, the biggest possible.

> **STARTING AROUND LUNCHTIME, I WOULD BE OFFICIALLY EQUAL TO OR BETTER THAN JOHN F. KENNEDY, GEORGE WASHINGTON, RONALD REAGAN, THOMAS JEFFERSON, ABE LINCOLN, ALL OF THE ROOSEVELTS.**

I was coming off a tough two years of running for president, of course, but also, believe it or not, a very tough two months as president-elect. There were a couple of really great days since the election, but only a couple. Such as—I think it was a Tuesday . . . hold on, I'll have one of the girls look it up. I want to be accurate. This is American history.

★ ★ ★ ★ ★ ★ ★ ★ ★ ★ ★ ★ ★ ★ ★ ★ ★ ★ ★ ★

I'M BACK. So this next part is like a flashback, okay?

It's December 19, 2016, a Monday morning, Christmas decorations all over Fifth Avenue. I'm in my incredible penthouse apartment on the 66th floor of Trump Tower in Manhattan—actually the 66th, 67th, *and* 68th floors: one for me, one for my beautiful wife, and one for our son, who I guess is probably my final child, which feels sad, almost like somebody died.

Trump Tower is legendary because of tenants like Donald Trump and The Trump Organization and Donald J. Trump for President Inc., but also because it's where Johnny Carson and Liberace lived and where Batman had his offices in *The Dark Knight Rises*, Wayne Enterprises. Also, while I'm thinking of it, Trump Tower disproves *all* the bad and unfair things people say about me. "Trump doesn't respect women"? The very first tenants in Trump Tower were Buccellati, great jewelry for women, and Charles Jourdan, great women's shoes. "Trump discriminates against the African Americans"? Michael Jackson lived on the sixty-third floor, same four-and-a-half-bath unit where I put my own parents. And Baby Doc, president of Haiti, black guy, had a beautiful place on the fifty-fourth floor. "Trump doesn't like the Hispanics and Latinos"? The owner of Jose Cuervo tequila owns three apartments! "Trump doesn't have a big heart, doesn't understand prison reform"? We've had many criminals living in Trump Tower, people who've paid their debts both to society and The Trump

Me, President-elect Trump,
at the Northern White House,
one of the great buildings on
earth, which I own.

Organization, and a couple actually served their house arrest sentences in their apartments!

So, anyway, I'm president-elect, it's December 19, 2016, Christmas season, beautiful, et cetera, and I stepped into my large private elevator with one of my Secret Service guys, the African American one, Anthony. Kanye West had visited me the week before, and I'd already asked Anthony a few times how much he'd love to "date" Kim Kardashian if he could — by which I meant a beautiful star, not a white girl, because I really am the least racist person I know, and besides, I don't believe Kim totally counts as white. Anyway, that morning instead I mentioned to Anthony I've lived in the apartment since 1984.

"Wow, sir, almost thirty-three years in the same home."

"And it looks exactly like it did when I moved in — same furniture, same beautiful marble, same everything, which is why I love it. I was Don Junior's age when I moved in, and now his oldest child is the same age as Barron, so it's like my own children are now the same age as me. Crazy, right?"

"Yes, sir. Kind of extraordinary."

"'*Extraordinary*' — good word, Anthony, very articulate word. Very high class."

"Thank you, sir."

"*Long* word." I counted. "Six syllables. As they call the parts of a word. You know, I'm Ivy League, I'm super intelligent, I know almost all of the words, except like some of the scientific ones, definitely all of the important ones, but the phonies, a lot of them, use too many long words like 'extraordinary' just to *sound* intelligent and rich. At Wharton I knew this guy James, you weren't supposed to call him Jim, come to think of it also an African American, very Sidney Poitier—'Good *evening*, Donald' and so forth. Not that you're a phony, Anthony—I mean, you really *look* a lot like Obama, but, you know, unlike him, with the white mother, I'm sure you kept it real growing up, the gangstas, the crack whores, all that; lucky to be alive and have a good government job now. Right?"

I enjoy talking to African Americans. I did extremely well with them in the election, about a hundred times as well as the pundits and fake polls said I would, which the media never wrote. Kanye told me he has almost as many followers as I do, which I don't really get, because he almost never tweets. I'm not saying he's lazy. But maybe the African American audience just isn't as demanding as my followers are.

At Trump Tower with my great African American Secret Service agent Anthony (and behind us, my great African American doorman).

We got off on twenty-six and I went to my office.

It was the day of my massive, massive landslide victory in the electoral college, which is the actual election that really counts and makes you president. Which was great, because I got a hundred more electoral votes than anybody ever thought I could, more than a hundred more. As many people know, I actually won the popular vote, too, even though the popular vote is just what in business we call a top-line number and really doesn't mean that much. Kellyanne Conway, my first counselor to the president, told me that in this whole century, in fact, the person elected president *doesn't* win the popular vote almost half the time. Which most people don't know. As many of my top people say, the popular vote is really kind of a straw poll, which is why there's an electoral college, to make the actual decision and keep out the losers and dopes—and crooks like you-know-who who gave tequila and food stamps to people from you-know-where to vote illegally in certain states.

But the great thing that happened concerning the electoral votes is the fantastic part that made me feel like I had truly, *truly* accomplished something outstanding. After the election, the Democrats continued trying to rig it against me right up to the end, pressured the people attending the electoral college to betray me and destroy tradition and break the law. But they failed so badly, because instead of going against *me*, almost all of the electoral college people who voted their "conscience" refused to vote for *Hillary*. It's true, look it up, even the fake media were forced to write about it because it was so amazing. And there were lots more in the college who *wanted* to vote against Hillary—maybe a hundred, nobody knows for sure—but they weren't allowed because the Democrats had rigged it. So the unfair tricks Hillary tried to set up to stop Trump? It hurt nasty, weak, crooked Hillary instead. It reminded me of when terrorists are building bombs but then accidentally blow themselves up. Which, every time it happens, makes me remember that God has got it all under control.

On December 19, 2016, I remember being so happy when Kellyanne rushed into my Trump Tower office to tell me about the Hillary defectors, happier than I'd been since the night of the election. In my mind at that moment, Hillary was suddenly even more of a shriveled-up and dying witch than she was on November 9, when my house crushed her, and her legs in a pantsuit curled up like in *The Wizard of Oz*. Now it was like the American people were all spitting on her, or something more disgusting, and she was melting, melting. So she's like both of the bad witches, but not Glinda. (My mother was like Glinda. My first two wives were like Glinda when I met them.) I asked everyone, "Do you think Hillary is literally *crying* right now?" They laughed even harder then, everyone except Jared, who smiles a lot in a way that looks sincere, but he never really laughs, which I find very impressive. Bannon made this gesture he does with his hand, underhanded, like he's clawing in and ripping out organs, always makes me chuckle. My "chief of staff," Reince Priebus, said he'd try to track down if Hillary really had cried when she heard the news. It was like the most beautiful, precious gift. "Merry Christmas!" I said. Everybody laughed. "And Happy Hanukkah, Jared," I added, with a wink, like I always do.

★ ★ ★ ★ ★ ★ ★ ★ ★

I WON, I'M A WINNER, I'M *THE* WINNER

T he one other big, big day between the election and the inauguration was January 6, a Friday. So as soon as I woke up I said "TGIF" out loud, which I've done every Friday since I was seven, even though my father called it a sissy thing and told me to stop, so for years I just mouthed it with my lips.

Right away I received an important and surprising piece of intelligence. I learned that five million Americans, actually less than five million, had watched the second episode of *The New Celebrity Apprentice*, starring Arnold Schwarzenegger, who can't be president, by the way, because both he and his parents were born in foreign countries. "Five million viewers," I said to Reince when I got down to the office, "probably the five million illegals who voted for Hillary." He chuckled, which bugged me. "I'm not joking, Reince." Then I received more intelligence — government stuff, classified — about the "hacking" of the insecure Democrat computers by whoever they let do that; all those e-mails from

Hillary's staff saying she's horrible—which, according to all the intelligence agencies, had no effect whatsoever on the election results, which actually surprised me, but whatever, fine. And somebody told me the FBI was investigating my national security adviser, Mike Flynn, because he's been working as a "lobbyist" for Turkey—because, under Obama, making a buck as a private citizen is against the law! Busy morning.

It was also the day that members of Congress—all of them together in that one big room, Congress Hall—actually opened and counted each one of my hundreds of electoral votes and legally certified my historic landslide victory, which meant that it was now completely real, as somebody said, "irreversible," or, as I thought, like when the loan documents on a deal are signed and sealed and no matter what might happen later, there was nothing they could do to take it away from me. We watched it on C-SPAN, which I'd never actually watched before. It's like cable news from the 1950s or in some foreign country. No close-ups. No action. No music. No ads. *So* boring. I'd told Speaker of the House Paul Ryan I really hoped he would stand up during the ceremony and hit the gavel and announce that of the seven electors who went off the reservation, *five* of them did it against *Hillary* and refused to vote for her, which was like the most ever, but I guess "protocol" prevented him. He'd told me he was worried that if he did that, some of his guys from the House might actually start chanting "*Lock her up.*" And I said: "You're '*worried*' about that?"

In the afternoon I had another nice piece of news that combined personal *and* presidential, which I've discovered is the very best. "Holistic," Ivanka calls things like that. We completed a deal for my personal lawyer's uncle-in-law—successful businessman, art dealer, real estate, grains, well connected, not a Russian, a *Ukrainian*, actually a *former* Ukrainian, an American citizen, stays in a condo down at our beautiful Trump Hollywood property, two hundred units right on the ocean—this guy Ivan, Alex, whatever, he's all set, starting that day, to help do a fabulous peace plan involving Europe. It's a peace plan the likes of which nobody's seen since World War II. It's still top secret so I can't go into the details. Actually, since I wasn't president back then on January 6, legally I *could* discuss the details, but I probably shouldn't. Maybe in a later chapter. And also, because I wasn't president yet, I was setting up that peace plan for *free*, as a gift to the American people. One more thing, by the way—even if I *had* been president at the time, and if I eventually made $10 billion from some amazing deal involving Europe—gas or oil or whatever—or $100 billion, it would

> **BECAUSE I WASN'T PRESIDENT YET, I WAS SETTING UP THAT PEACE PLAN FOR *FREE*, AS A GIFT TO THE AMERICAN PEOPLE.**

be totally fine, because it's legally impossible for a president to have any conflict of interest, according to the Constitution. Which is surprising, but so great, because our presidents have enough to worry about without getting all caught up in technicalities. It's the kind of little-known but really fantastic item that makes me respect our brilliant Founders so greatly and feel so proud to be an American.

★ ★

IVANKA JUST OVERHEARD that last part and reminded me to mention that January 6 was *also* her little brother Eric's thirty-third birthday, and also the day we found out his wife was pregnant with my ninth grandchild. So that probably made it a very nice day, too. Because, quite frankly, Eric has been married for two, two and a half years, so Don Junior and I had already started with the funny "shooting blanks" sound effects, plus his wife is at least a couple of years older than Eric, not exactly a young woman.

★ ★

THOSE WERE THE TWO top-of-the-line days between November 9 and January 20, the only two out of like a hundred. I
figured that the two months of being president-elect would be two
of my best months of all time—*I won, I'm a winner, I'm the winner, millions of people excited about me, millions of people scared
of me, I'm on vacation.* But those two months were, quite frankly,
two of the most boring of my life. In fact, I must tell you, one of
the major, major challenges of being president that nobody has
ever talked about or even known, not even historians—until now,
because I'm being totally honest with you—is how *boring* the
job is so much of the time. And not *just* boring, the way talking
to some applicant from South Dakota for farming secretary is
boring, but also so many complicated explanations you have to
hear, unbelievably complicated—math, history, legal, all of it. I
mean, I'm a smart guy, graduated Wharton top of my class, great
at accounting, math, but you wouldn't believe the boring. And so
many long meetings, listening to these know-it-alls, the grinds
and geeks and "experts." I've never been a big meetings or "experts"
guy. I do my best to make being president exciting, the way it's
supposed to be, but it takes work, trust me, and it takes Trump.

I did hire a fantastic cabinet, probably the best cabinet in American history, certainly the best one since we were a country separate from England. But getting there was a job the likes of which
I wouldn't wish on anybody. I conducted an unbelievable number of interviews, at least a hundred, possibly a thousand, a truly
crazy number. Hiring the cabinet was like casting the candidates
for *The Apprentice* and *The Celebrity Apprentice*, NBC's most
successful show of the twenty-first century, but compressing what
we did over fifteen years into *two months*. And at least a lot of the
people back then, casting *The Apprentice*, were very attractive
women; for the record, I was unmarried until the end of the second
season. And unlike with the shows, until January 20, 2017, I

wasn't even getting paid! I was working totally *pro bono*, pardon my French. And so was Jared, working for those two months on very important and very secret arrangements with some major international players to bring peace to Syria, among other major, major things that will make America great.

I am a strong believer in sitting down personally with the people dying to work for me—eye to eye, face-to-face, kick the tires, give them the smell test. And the smell part I mean literally. For instance, when I first met Steve Bannon in 2011, I thought, "Hey, come on, the khaki slacks and the no necktie and the big gut and spotty face—quite frankly reminded me of the actor Broderick Crawford kind of imitating Truman Capote. But then I got a whiff off Steve of this certain *aroma* that winners have that I'm able to smell. It's hard to describe, and other people can't smell it, but it's kind of peppermint plus leather plus electrical fire or butane, but nicer, more like air-conditioning. If you believe in superpowers, which I found out a lot of people do—the Christians, the charismatics, *love* the charismatics—then smelling winners is one of my superpowers. Speaking of those, I sometimes feel like Steve can almost read my mind, like how my mom knew when my dad wanted to smack me, or how Aquaman could talk to all the sea creatures underwater. Sometimes I'll be trying to put a complicated idea into words and Steve suddenly says exactly what I'm thinking. One night when the two of us were alone in the Oval Office and he said a guy thing about Hope Hicks, my fantastic twenty-eight-year-old PR girl—so good-looking, so loyal, doesn't gossip—it was almost like he was one of those magic ventriloquist dummies from *The Twilight Zone*.

You probably don't realize that there are like twenty-five individual cabinet members, plus fifteen or twenty other "cabinet-level" positions, where a lot of my fantastic women are, such as Mrs. Mitch McConnell, who's also Chinese, which is great. (I mean, even Reince Priebus is technically cabinet level, which makes me smile every time I think of it, but good for Reince. Also, Reince needs Secret Service protection? I thought they were kidding me the first time they told me that. And *Reince*: Weird name, right? You have to force your mouth into a funny fish-face just even to say it. And *Priebus*, for that matter—he swears it's German, but I don't know, because I'm very familiar with the German names and that's not like one I ever heard.) And that's not even counting the guys up for Supreme Court who met with me at Trump Tower but were all secretly brought in, I think some in disguises, one possibly dressed as a woman.

It was extremely hard work, all those interviews, one after another, most of them the kind of people I've never spent more than ninety seconds with at a time. Although because the offices and conference rooms on the twenty-sixth floor of the Tower are all fitted out with the very best A/V equipment, we now have fantastic high-def video of all my meetings with all the finalists for the cabinet, for the Supreme Court, for embassies, for every-thing. Plus all of the phone conversations I personally placed to the losers. Such fantastic stuff, dramatic *and* funny *and* historic. And sometimes truly moving. It was Bannon who actually told Chris Christie he was out as head of the transition team—that was in Trump Tower, and we've got this *amazing* zoom-in on Chris's face where he uses his tie to wipe away the tears. Later on, picking my cabinet, I phoned Chris with the heads-up he wasn't the right fit for any of the varsity jobs, and on that tape you can hear him choke up. "C'mon, Chrissy," I say, "the surgery is starting to work, and if you get down to 250, 225, we can defi-nitely see if there's an opening in 2018, 2019." (He's been texting me every time he loses a couple more pounds. Cute.) Anyhow, every one of them signed waivers giving us permission to use any records of those meetings and conversations in any way we wanted, so Mark Burnett has actually started putting together a season of *Ultimate American Apprentice* before we hand over the material to the Donald J. Trump Presidential Library and All-American

Golf Resort™, and eventually also to the National Archives. I can't wait for you to see it.

Unfortunately, we only have audio of Mitt Romney from his interview to be secretary of state, because I did that one in public, so the whole world could see. People say no president-elect ever did anything so transparent. (Although for the show, Burnett says we can do an over-the-shoulder two-shot of me and an *actor* playing Mitt, with me reenacting my lines and Mitt's authentic original ones dubbed in.) Our meeting took place at Jean-Georges, in my hotel overlooking Central Park, maybe probably the best restaurant on earth—Trump *International* Hotel, beautiful giant silver globe of the Earth out front, *international* restaurant; chef has a French first name and a German last name, perfect place to discuss secretary of state. My idea.

It was right around Thanksgiving, which I understand the Mormons do not celebrate as a religious holiday. I was mostly doing it as a courtesy to Mitt, letting him apologize in person for what he'd said a few months earlier—that "dishonesty is Donald Trump's hallmark," that I'm "a fraud" who's all about "the bullying, the greed, the showing off, the misogyny, the absurd third-grade theatrics." I must tell you, I began with serious doubts about somebody who talks like Professor Thurston

HE SUDDENLY REMINDED ME OF OTTER IN *ANIMAL HOUSE*, SO I FELT FORGIVING. AND SECRETARY OF ENERGY: WHO CARES?

Howell III—"misogyny," "absurd theatrics," please. And really, would we want somebody who, after saying that crap, comes groveling for a job that doesn't even have much real power? Very weak. Very sad. (Rick Perry called me a "carnival act" and "a cancer" back in 2015, but he's not some Harvard phony like Mitt—when Rick recently said to me privately and very sincerely, "Donald, Mr. President-elect, the darned truth is I'm just not as smart as you," he suddenly reminded me of Otter in *Animal House*, so I felt forgiving. And secretary of energy: Who cares?)

Mitt *looks* like he could be a winner, I know, central casting, but he just doesn't smell like a winner. Certain members of my own family are similar, quite frankly. By the way, Mitt drank a Diet Coke before our dinner, which surprised me, since I know that's a sin for Mormons. Also? After dinner in the men's room— *gorgeous* restrooms at Jean-Georges, by the way—he refused to arm wrestle me, and then I couldn't even hear his stream hitting the porcelain. (Neither could Anthony, my African American Secret Service man.) That is an actual scientific sign of weakness, I'm afraid, a medical fact I got from Dr. Oz personally.

"Not good," I told Reince on the ride back to Trump Tower. "Not a winner. But quite frankly, I do really, really love the *look* of Mitt. Who's got that look but also true toughness, and a strong *stream*?" Reince brought up Bob Corker, the senator from Kentucky or Mississippi, one of those. "I don't love the hair," I said, "his name's like a joke, and he's even shorter than you, Reince." A week later at Trump Tower, when Rex Tillerson was in front of me—standing beside me, actually, a hydrant, like a minute ten—I knew I had my man.

Although, can I say something about those job titles? *Secretary* of state, *secretary* of this, *secretary* of that. It's not prestigious, not respectful. Even your actual *secretary* you're now supposed to call your assistant, right? Well, we're going to fix that, because guess what: I discovered "secretary" *isn't in the Constitution*, which nobody really realized, so starting very soon we're changing all the job titles. Secretary of state and treasury secretary and defense secretary become EVP International, EVP Finance, and EVP International Security. We make HUD secretary our SVP Buildings and Grounds, Cities; and interior secretary becomes SVP Buildings and Grounds, Rural; and secretary of commerce will be SVP Business Development; and so forth. More clear, much more dignified. Mike Pence was a little iffy about the SVPs and EVPs, but I told him the Constitution ties my hands on what we call him—but then I had the idea of always calling him *the* vice president, emphasize the word "the," which calmed him down. Good guy, Mike. And I also told him sure, if it's important to him, he can be my official White House "prayer warrior," too.

Across from the Northern White House on Fifth Avenue, greeting Trump supporters, who would still support me even if I shot one of them.

★ ★ ★ ★ ★ ★ ★ ★ ★

WITH GREAT WEALTH COMES GREAT QUALITY

S o now we're completely done with the flashback sequences, totally back to *now*—Friday, January 20, 2017, Inauguration Day. Earlier this week I finally picked the last member of the cabinet, I honestly can't recall right now which one—one of the second-stringers—Department of Transportation Safety, maybe Mining and Agricultural Services Department, one of those, you can look it up. But all my direct reports are hired and I'm *done*.

Speaking of my cabinet, after the photo deal with the Obamas at the White House, just as we were gathering in the Capitol, one of my cabinet guys giggled—I won't say who, don't want the PC police coming down on him, but he is a naughty little pixie. I made him show me the text he was looking at on his phone. "Congratulations on being part of America's first un-nig-uration!" and then it has one of those Japanese cell phone cartoons: a monkey with his hands over his ears. I disavowed it then and there—"Hey," I said. But it's also free speech, which is a very important Trump issue. And it's their culture, and it's important Alabama historical material, so it belongs here in the book. If I pulled a Nixon and erased things that aren't necessarily PC, then the unfair media would be hitting me for *that*, right?

All of the presidents except the original Bush, who's ninety-two and supposedly too sick to make the trip, attended my inauguration—even Jimmy Carter, who's also ninety-two and could have used his cancer as an excuse. In fact, Carter was the very first to RSVP, which I feel was his way of apologizing for saying during the campaign that Trump "rejects the most important moral and ethical principles on which our nation was founded." Bill Clinton came with Hillary, of course, which they had to do, or else she would have looked even more like a tired and unwell loser grandma. (Bill: so thin, so pale, I said, "Hey, buddy, start eating *steak* again, for crying out loud." Poor Bill—that diet, that wife. Good chance that as president I'll be asked to speak at his funeral, which will be a great honor. Also probably Carter's and the old Bush's.) When Hillary arrived for the ceremony at the Capitol, the crowd actually booed—I didn't hear it, because I was still backstage, but Kellyanne sent me one of those video jiffies of the footage, which I'm actually watching right now on my phone. The way it repeats over and over is what makes it funny. I had to force myself to stop watching it.

Then there was my speech. Remember when Obama surprised everybody by singing "Amazing Grace" at that very sad black funeral in the South? People loved that. *Loved* it. My idea was to end my inauguration speech by saying, as I did, "America will start winning again, winning like never before." But then suddenly the music would come up and I would start *singing*—"We . . . are . . . the . . . champions, no time for losers, 'cause we are the champions of the world!" Boom, people are going wild, applauding, screaming, crying. Would've been amazing. But Mike Pence literally *pleaded* with me not to do that, because it turns out the guy who sang it originally was gay.

My fallback idea was to end the inauguration speech with the lines, "I will never, ever let you down. The forgotten men and women of our country will be forgotten no longer. See how they run, like pigs from a gun? Everyone is listening to you now." Then, cue the U.S. Army band, music up, and I *sing* "I am he as you are me and we are all together!" and repeat it over and over, easier to sing than the Queen song, clapping my hands, everyone joins in, then I'm like, "God bless you, and God bless America!" Boom, the end, totally upbeat after Bannon's "carnage" stuff earlier. But Ivanka didn't get the Beatles reference, so in the end I decided to play it straight. As it turned out, people said the speech was one of the five best of all time.

Next time, 2021, I'm going to put back in the line Ivanka and Jared cut from this one: "I'm the richest president America has ever had—which I don't say to brag about being wealthy, but because the next five richest presidents are Kennedy, Washington, Jefferson, Teddy Roosevelt, and Andrew Jackson—three of the four on Mount Rushmore plus Trump plus Trump 1.0 (Jackson)! As the proverb says, 'With great wealth comes great quality, the best.'" And my second inaugural will definitely have more pizzazz, more like Super Bowl halftime, maybe I sing "My Way" from the open door of Marine One as we hover over the Capitol dome, a couple of U.S. Marines on either side of me firing American flags at the crowd out of T-shirt canons. That was actually Barron's great idea. Kellyanne says one of the marines should be an African American gal. Fine.

★ ★ ★ ★ ★ ★ ★ ★ ★ ★

THE ACTUAL LEGAL TAKEOVER OF THE GOVERNMENT

M y inauguration, the actual legal takeover of the government with the Bible and then the speech, felt totally fantastic. Everybody watching, everybody listening, not just the two or three million there on the Mall but like a billion people all over America and all over the world, on TV and online—probably on radio in Africa and India—so many watching, so many listening, no laughing, no talking (just me talking), total respect, even the haters terrified into a kind of respect, everyone focused on President Donald J. Trump. It would've been perfect if I hadn't had to *read* the speech, because reading always brings down my mood, both in public out loud and by myself. But they wouldn't let me wing it. Still, incredible, amazing, phenomenal.

But that was, what, seventeen minutes? My Inauguration *Day* lasted seventeen *hours*, and I must tell you, most of it was a waste of time and fake. That lunch with all the supposed Washington VIPs and "leaders" in the Capitol Rotunda? Terrible acoustics, acoustics from 1776 or whenever, acoustics that wouldn't even be allowed in construction today. That event was a great example of why, until I came along, the American people were completely bored by politicians and government. Went on forever, with the president, me, just sitting there listening to other people say all their phony things, so dull—except when I told Hillary to stand and get a round of applause. Although I didn't mean for *everyone else* to stand, like an ovation, but fine, whatever, nice moment, presidential, I'm a gentleman, she lost so badly and surprisingly everybody knows she's permanently humiliated; I didn't need to rub it in right then.

One thing I've always known is that the great *ups* in life never last very long. Usually not even a minute, often just a few seconds. It's "*Oh, yeah!*"—and then, gone, bye-bye, not happy anymore. It's true after you put out a great tweet. It's true after you have that great moment with someone you love. It's true after you eat a great dessert, like the superb three-layer Trump chocolate cake at the Mar-a-Lago Club. I guess I was lucky to learn this lesson young. In fact, learning it is my earliest memory, and it also involves cake. My third birthday party, fantastic time, leaning over the Carvel cake to blow out the candles, my hair catches on fire. Mom yells "Fred, *no*" just as Dad pushes my face into the cake to put it out and starts laughing like a maniac, one of the only times I remember him laughing. The other thing I know is that you always remember the *downs* much, much more clearly and much, much longer than the *ups*, like each one is one of those video jiffies from Twitter playing over and over and over in your mind, and you can't delete them.

Now I'm president. I won. I *won*. *I* won. My first morning at the White House. Day One.

> *VOICE MEMO: Presidential to-do list*
> *Song, "I WON / I WON / DAY ONE," © 2017 by*
> *Donald J. Trump.*

Sorry. I've been president since yesterday, so I guess this is Day Two. But it's a Saturday, so we'll say Monday is Day One. This weekend is the warm-up, like hitting a few balls before you actually tee off. (Funny story: Before we were married, I'd said that as a "figure of speech" many times privately to the First Lady before she was First Lady, when we were alone, in the dark—and then when she heard me use it literally for the first time at a Trump golf course, with other people around, she didn't understand what I meant and got very embarrassed.) Anyhow, it's Day One Minus Two of the President Trump Administration, and what do I wake up to? All of the disgusting, dishonest media lying about the size of the crowd at my inauguration, every channel, every so-called expert. It was like bringing a beautiful supermodel home at night: You're so happy, but then the next morning there's a rotting corpse in bed. (Another figure of speech. Although that did also actually happen to a friend of mine.)

Why did I care so much about the totally wrong and fake crowd estimates? I didn't care for *myself*, I'm used to that, I've had thirty years of that kind of rude treatment by the vicious media. What I really cared about, as Kellyanne explained to me, were the feelings of the millions of people who traveled from all over America and stood for hours to experience the most sacred moment of their lives. I was angry, as Bannon explained to me, on behalf of the forgotten men and women the elite media wanted to keep forgotten, to erase them from the historical record with their Big Lie. Reince said we could maybe create a federal Office of Crowd Size Measurement in the Commerce Department, because they're already in charge of the atomic clock that controls time. Which, by the way, I'm pretty sure my brilliant MIT engineer uncle, Dr. John Trump, invented.

★ ★

IN THE LIMO THIS MORNING on the way out to the CIA, Kellyanne gave me a neck rub, the way Ivanka used to love doing when she was little, and then I felt even better when I delivered a great speech to the staff there. They gave me several amazing standing ovations. If I were the type of guy who cried, I think I would have felt like crying. But then afterward, on the way out, somebody told me CIA headquarters is now officially called the George Bush Center for Intelligence. At first I thought that was some kind of Washington insider joke, but it turns out they mean the old Bush, Grandpa Bush, who it turns out ran the CIA for a year. Which suddenly made me put two and two together and realize why all the intelligence big shots are against me since I destroyed Jeb Bush, knocked him out of the race a week after the first primary even though he spent $150 million against me. *I get it now*, I thought to myself as

BUT WHEN REINCE AND KELLYANNE BOTH LOOKED AT ME FUNNY, I REALIZED I'D SAID ALL THAT OUT LOUD. BUT I DIDN'T APOLOGIZE, OR REFER TO IT, JUST LOOKED STRAIGHT AHEAD. WHICH IS LEADERSHIP 101.

we sat down in the limo for the ride back to D.C., *it's why Billy Bush secretly taped me a decade ago. It's Hillary and Obama and the media and intelligence and the Bushes all in a giant circle jerk, and I'm tied down on the ground in the middle, and it's disgusting.* But when Reince and Kellyanne both looked at me funny, I realized I'd said all that out loud. But I didn't apologize, or refer to it, just looked straight ahead. Which is Leadership 101.

"You know," I said, "out here we're already halfway to Trump National." That's my luxurious world-class club in Virginia, two beautiful courses. "We can stop in McLean for Big Macs, Oreo McFlurries, whatever you guys want, on me. Hey, Anthony, Kanye told me McDonald's is his favorite brand! We grab a bite, then we hit a few balls to work it off."

Nobody said anything.

"What? There's no snow on the ground. *What?*"

"Mr. President," Kellyanne said, "the media would kill us if you played golf the first day."

"What if I played with Anthony? And let them take pictures? It'd be great, special commemoration of Martin Luther King month. You play, Anthony? Maybe caddied when you were young?"

"I do play, Mr. President, but we aren't allowed to on duty."

"They let you jog with the joggers and bike with the bicyclists but not golf with the golfers? So elitist. Reince, have Jeffy Sessions look into that."

"The Secret Service has never been in Justice, Mr. President, and it's part of Homeland Security now."

"I know, of course I know that, but I think it's very stupid and disorganized and it should be with the FBI. But okay, fine, better, we don't need to talk to Comey about golfing. Anthony, you know you're probably lucky you don't work for Comey at the FBI. Such a loose cannon."

I let Reince try the neck rub, but it didn't help at all—turns out he's a pincher, way too fast and nervous and hard. "He's harming the president," I said to Anthony. "Stop him." Everybody chuckled, which didn't please me. Then the video jiffy of liars on the news shows laughing about my inauguration crowd started playing in my head again. I told Kellyanne that Sean Spicer needed to round up the reporters at the White House—I didn't care if it *was* late Saturday afternoon, none of them do the "Shabbat"—and tell them yesterday's inauguration crowd was the largest outdoor

As Ivanka discusses important things
with her fellow top West Wing aides,
I practice my special new *Olympus
Has Fallen White House Down* Code Red
Commander in Chief Escape Plan.

audience of any kind in the history of America, maybe in the world, and probably visible from the moon. She said, "How about 'biggest inauguration crowd ever'?" and I okayed that. Trump isn't unreasonable.

When I got back to the White House, I didn't want to watch them lie on CNN, and during the day between *Fox & Friends* and prime-time, TV is pretty boring, especially on Saturdays, so I used the time to really inspect the place. I don't want to complain or criticize. It's the White House. Historic, Washington, Lincoln, Kennedy, Marilyn, et cetera. Ultraexclusive. I'm sure I'll get used to it, but it's not what I would do, in terms of furnishings, fixtures, and finishes. It's elegant, but it's not twenty-first-century super-deluxe. The limestones, the marbles—there's actually not much stone in the White House, and it's all white or off-white or gray or black, very bland. The building is 217 years old, which is older than I personally prefer in a residential facility. My personal taste is luxurious and Continental, what Ivanka calls "more Abu Dhabi, less Alabama"—no offense, Jeffy Sessions, you Alabama pixie. I've heard people say the White House style is kind of stodgy and somewhat rustic, not very fun, because it's the kind of house a lot of WASP snobs have, horsey people with the fake English accents whose great-grandfather maybe had a lot of money but now it's all gone. Although to be fair, on the floor above the ground floor there's a nice big hallway—double-high ceiling, big columns, good chandeliers, *almost* Trump.

My actual private living area in the White House is much, much smaller than I'm used to—20,000 square feet, which I know sounds big, but my penthouse in Trump Tower is *30,000*, okay? The *entire* White House, including all the servant barracks or whatever that I haven't even seen yet, is half as big as Mar-a-Lago. I'm not even exaggerating. The Oval Office is very special, great branding, iconic. Nice high ceiling. But I literally have bigger *bathrooms* in my homes. At least they've already put up the new gold drapes I

picked in the Oval, which look so much more strong and sophisticated than the cheap red ones Obama had in there. Everybody
tells me I can't be the first president to install a TV in the Oval.
"Why can't I?" I said when we first walked in on Friday. "The
American people would love me for it. We could hang a pair of
small screens, thirty inches, forty inches, either side of the big
window there, behind the desk, where those paintings are. TVs
are just the better, modern version of paintings, right?" They said
maybe later, after the first hundred days.

For views you've got the lawns and the Washington Monument,
which are okay, but in Trump Tower you're next to Central Park,
which is about a hundred times as big, with lakes, and we don't
even need to pay a cent for the gardening. And at Mar-a-Lago,
exactly the same size grounds as the White House but you've got
views of both the *mar*, which is the Spanish for "ocean," and the
lago, which means "Intracoastal Waterway."

I already know the White House will never really feel like home.
Not because it's temporary, but because I don't *own* it. The
Southern White House, Mar-a-Lago, I *own*. I *own* Trump Tower.
The people who work at my homes work *for me*, not for the
government. I could tear down Trump Tower and Mar-a-Lago if
I wanted, I could fire anyone on the staffs for no reason at all,
and they'd be out on their ass, not just transferred to a new job
in some government cafeteria somewhere. (At least I have my
old friend Keith right next to me, my bodyguard for twenty
years, ex-NYPD detective, now director of Oval Office opera-

CALL ME SENTIMENTAL, BUT IT MAKES ME SAD THAT I'LL NEVER *OWN* THE WHITE HOUSE.

tions, which means he's with me forty hours a week but off my
personal payroll, so win-win.) Call me sentimental, but it makes
me sad that I'll never *own* the White House. I've been told that

my sons Donald Junior and Eric, who now operate our company independently, offered to pay $430 million in cash for the entire White House complex. It would be an unofficial property in the award-winning Trump Hotel Collection™, with the East Wing refitted for four or eight years as a members-only White House Club, and the White House and West Wing practically *donated* to the government for four or eight years with a buyback option at the end. All of which was not my sons' idea originally, by the way, although they realize it's brilliant. We—by that I mean The Trump Organization, which I do not currently control at all—had an amazing guy in Kyrgyzstan, great country, totally ready to make the purchase loan, but the deal was too sophisticated for the government lawyers and bean counters to understand. In fact, it was their obsolete approach on that amazing opportunity that made me agree that we should create the White House Office of American Innovation, run by Jared Kushner, my young, innovative, et cetera, son-in-law.

Not that Don Junior and Eric and The Trump Organization need the White House, because I've heard they're now doing a major hotel expansion all over America, and although I don't know any of the details whatsoever or the local regulatory or loan situations or anything like that, people are saying that one of the hotel deals they're doing is in Valley Forge, which would be so perfect, so special—Washington slept here then, Trump sleeps here now, the one who made America, the one who made America great again, et cetera. The ads would write themselves.

★ ★ ★ ★ ★ ★ ★ ★ ★

I NEED A TV
IN THE OVAL

Reince reminds me of the nice kid in high school who manages the sports team but the players never hang out with. He actually trots around the White House, runs down the halls, I guess to make it look like he's dealing with important emergency situations as my chief of staff. Somewhat cute, somewhat sad. "With Reince around," Bannon says, "you really don't *need* a dog here." Yesterday when Steve and Kellyanne and I walked out of the Oval, Reince suddenly popped out of one of the boardrooms and ran up right behind us. Steve barked like a dog and said, "See Reince run! *Run*, Reince, *run*!" and we all cracked up.

By the way? No dogs in the Trump White House. The breath, the drool, the funguses, the parasites, the disease, the feces, the claws, the barking. Never. I haven't touched a live animal since I was eleven years old. For me it's what they call a core principle.

Anyway, this morning, on Day . . . one-two-three-*four*, Day Four of my administration, at 8-something, almost 9—I know the time because I'd just switched from *Fox & Friends* during the final ad break to *Morning Joe*—Reince ran into the little private "dining room" next to the Oval Office, which has a television, tiny, unbelievably small, but at least it means I don't have to go all the way upstairs to watch. Ordered a 65-inch this morning, also getting a big, big, big crystal chandelier. A president needs a TV in the Oval, he really does.

Multitasking in the Oval Office: watching fantastic Steve Doocy and the other guy and the blonde on *Fox & Friends* while my aides and "experts" brief me.

"Mr. President," Reince said, "one of . . . those calls just came into the switchboard."

On the first Sunday, the president of Belarus had tried to call me directly at the White House but didn't go through the State Department, so the operator refused to put him through. Very bad. Belarus is actually an important little nation, which most people don't know, right between Germany and Russia, now independent, very independent, strategic. Bigger than England. According to Mike Flynn, who knows Mr. Lukashenko, he felt very disrespected. So I told Reince: *Always* let me know whenever a call like that comes through.

"Who is it? Presidente Piñata calling back to say he's coming after all?" Jared arranged to bring the Mexican president up to talk about the Wall he's paying for, but he just canceled. It reminds me of what a lot of people in the construction and hospitality industries say about workers of certain backgrounds who call in at the last minute and say "Sorry, boss, mañana." (By the way, Piñata is actually the president's name, so I'm not being "racist.")

"No," Reince told me, "it's a guy who is supposedly Kim Jong-un and his translator from the UN. The call did originate on the Korean peninsula, translator on a second line in New York, but the duty officer in the Situation Room thinks it's almost certainly not the Supreme Leader of North Korea."

"'*Almost* certainly,' huh?" It was Presidential Decision Time. This could be my chance for the most important peace deal ever: Trump saves the world on *Day Four*. "I was 'almost certainly' gonna lose to Hillary, remember? Put him through! But go get Steve, I want a grown-up in here."

I've done business with the Koreans, and right away I really thought I was hitting it off with the guy. Warmed him up at first, told him getting rid of his uncle, brother, and some of the disloyal generals—*boom*—that was very smart, very necessary, showed everybody he was boss. I said it's great he's young, at his age I built my first hotel and started Trump Tower, and I also told him my first movie star crush as a kid was a Kim—Kim Novak. Then I turned a little tough. "None of us want the nuclear, right, Kim, Mr. Kim, Supreme Leader?" I said. And he agreed. "You've got, what, twenty nukes?" I asked. "And can shoot one all the way to Japan, maybe, on a good day? And I've got like six *thousand—*" Bannon held up four fingers. "*Four thousand* warheads, the finest missiles, all aimed at you if I want—*kaboom*, sayonara! Not that I do want that. At all. So let's talk, let's figure out what makes us both happy campers."

He spoke Korean, and then after a couple of minutes his translator suddenly referred to me as "President-*erect* Trump, you *velly* erect." I realized it was my son Eric doing his Oriental voice. The "Kim" guy was a Georgetown buddy of Eric's, an actual South Korean who works in marketing at our magnificent Daewoo Trump World condominium property in Seoul. "You got me!" I said. Reince and Steve were a little P-O'd, but I told them they shouldn't be—it was a good dress rehearsal for the real thing.

★ ★ ★ ★ ★ ★ ★ ★ ★ ★ ★ ★ ★ ★ ★ ★ ★ ★ ★ ★

THAT PREMIERE WEEK I took my first flight on Marine One and Air Force One, up and back from Philadelphia. I'm sure for other presidents having the use of a big private jet is one of the most amazing parts of the job—the thing that really makes them almost feel, temporarily, like a Donald Trump. Air Force One was fine, but again, like the White House, I don't *own* her. The 747 is a much, much more old-fashioned model than my Trump 757. The engines aren't Rolls-Royce, like on my beautiful 650-miles-per-hour T-Bird, and of course it doesn't have the very famous 24-karat gold bathroom fixtures. They say Air Force One can fly over a nuclear blast and survive. We'll see.

THEY SAY AIR FORCE ONE CAN FLY OVER A NUCLEAR BLAST AND SURVIVE. WE'LL SEE.

I was only in Philly for an hour, giving a pep talk to the Republicans from Congress—I guess for those guys a couple of nights out of town at a Loews is a real treat—but I also used the time in flight to sign papers, so many papers, all the executive orders and what not. Although I do like saying "by the authority vested in me as president by the Constitution and laws of the United States of America" out loud. A lot about being president reminds me of what my very underrated Oscar-nominated friend and supporter Gary Busey told me about being a movie star. "You do your art for twenty minutes, and then instead of kicking back the rest of the day, all these dweebs you barely know are yakking at you and shoving documents at you." Gary wants to be ambassador to the Virgin Islands. I'd love to make that happen for him.

Some of the papers you sign really matter. I spent the whole flight back to Washington reading the big one—every word, thousands of words. It was the one "Protecting the Nation from Foreign Terrorist Entry into the United States." Who wouldn't want that, right? And I should get a little credit, quite frankly, for having made the ban nicer than some people wanted it to be—no ban on people from Indonesia or Turkey, no ban on people from Saudi Arabia or Dubai, which between them is like half the Muslims in the world. Although why would anybody from Dubai become a terrorist? Fantastic place, no dirty factories, although I love manufacturing, everything brand-new, especially the Trump International Golf Club, biggest clubhouse in Dubai, which I've been told my sons are officially opening next month, and coming soon will be the Trump World Golf Club, designed by Tiger Woods, one of my close African American friends. Love the Tiger. "You're *grrrrreat!*" I tell him whenever we get together.

As we landed at Andrews, I congratulated my team for writing up the executive order without even one mention of Muslim or Islamic or Arab or whatever. Very smart. I asked if that was modeled on the voter ID thing, right, where the laws the Republicans passed in the states never actually *mention* blacks or Mexicans, they're just, "Hey, we want better vetting at the voting booth." Reince and Kellyanne and everybody just smiled. Because if they said anything, they know the dishonest PC media might use it against them somehow. I get that.

★ ★ ★ ★ ★ ★ ★ ★ ★

IT FINALLY FELT REAL, LIKE A MOVIE

My second weekend as president, I really *felt* like *the president*. It finally felt *real*, like a movie. Or I guess since it was live, more like one of those Broadway shows based on a movie, like *The Color Purple* or *School of Rock*, except not a musical. It got very exciting, because it wasn't just signing the papers and posing for the pictures.

I called Piñata, told him he'd better stop saying he's not paying for the Wall, and I might have to send our military in to take care of his drug guys. And by the way, that I hadn't really enjoyed my trip down to see him last summer. "*Burn.*" Cut!

Then I called the prime minister of Australia and gave it to *him* straight—*we're* supposed to take *your* refugees from terrorist countries? You can tie me kangaroo down, sport. Cut! After Iran shoots off a missile test, I tell them (and my millions and millions of other followers on Twitter) that they have been PUT ON

NOTICE, just like that, in all capital letters—and the weak Obama and Hillary holdovers in the State Department can't believe their eyes. Cut!

Friday night I had the FBI director over for an early dinner at the White House, just the two of us, Comey and me—asked him if he liked how nice I was to him when he was here for an event a few days before, the hug, public hug from Trump, told him I was glad he liked his job so much and that I'd heard he's a very loyal guy, especially to bosses, very chain-of-command guy, and I assumed he'd always give any boss a heads-up if the boss were ever under investigation, especially if the investigation was some total hoax. Close-up on my face, close-up on his face, he tells me I'm *not* under investigation, *cut!*

I called another CEO to tell him if he kept his factory open in Iowa or Indiana, someplace, at least for a while, we'd make it very strongly worth his while. And that if he built a factory in Mexico, his children and grandchildren would regret it—and no, I said, I didn't mean "future generations of Americans," I meant *his* children and grandchildren.

If he didn't believe me, I told this guy, check out the trouble the Tic Tac company is facing after the *Access Hollywood* tape incident. The president of the United States gives their product the greatest publicity they've ever had, and then put out a statement calling me "unacceptable"?

By the way, here's some revealing personal information, which I know is the kind of thing people love in books like this. After I decided I was quitting Tic Tacs last fall, Chris Christie sent over a whole basket of new fresheners for me to try—Breath Savers, Mentos, Certs, Dentyne Mints, Listerine PocketMist, Binaca. *Binaca* he found somewhere! They probably still sell it in Jersey. Came out when I was a kid, went through like one a week back then. Ivanka and Jared suggested Altoids. I thought, *"Original Celebrated Curiously Strong Mints," give me a break, so gay, so elitist, also not American, British.* But Rex Tillerson told me they're actually made by Kraft or Wrigley, totally American. So for now I'm an Altoids guy.

Anyhow, that second weekend as president, my ban on terrorists was also going into effect—our border guys at the airports kicking ass and taking names. Literally! Sending possible terrorists back to Timbuktu after checking them for bombs! (Interesting fact not many people know: Timbuktu—actual place in Africa, Islamic.)

It even added to the drama having all the protesters and lawyers fighting us, which I'm used to—another way I'm more prepared for this job than other presidents when they've come in, part of the real beauty of Trump. That weekend was like when demolition finally starts on a major, major new Trump property, after the architects and engineers have been planning for months and years. And sometimes you go ahead even when you don't have every single *t* crossed and *i* dotted on the permits and "environmental impact statements" and so forth, you just go, go, go. Unlike with a building, we didn't have months or years to plan this all out, because I was only president for a week. So I guess it was less like a construction project and more like when you realize the girl you just met is a little buzzed and willing to go all the way, and there's like this formality of small talk where you're smiling but you're afraid she might pass out or cry or something so you just, you know, go in. What I mean is, not so much planning.

Mad Dog Mattis wished we'd given him and the Pentagon more of a heads-up on the ban, but I really, really didn't want the terrorists to have any warning so they could pull their refugee disguises together. I think I convinced Mad Dog I was right about that. He didn't tell me I wasn't. And General Kelly's guys at Homeland

Security didn't know it was coming either, but I think it's good to keep your own people on their toes. Right? You don't tell employees in advance about a drug test. Or like when you don't always tell the wife ahead of time that tonight's the night, until suddenly, *bam*, it is, therefore she always has to be ready to do what needs doing. Leadership 101.

Sunday morning Jared came over to the White House to watch the shows with me—Jared is family, so we were upstairs in the private presidential "living room," which is small, more like a den than a living room—and discussed the terrorist ban. When things started hitting the fan on Friday night and all day Saturday, Jared wasn't around, which was fine, and he couldn't even talk with me on the phone, which was fine, or text or e-mail, which I don't do anyway.

HE IS VERY, VERY, VERY JEWISH, WHICH I RESPECT SO MUCH, HE'S BASICALLY IN JEWISH JAIL FROM FRIDAY THROUGH SATURDAY NIGHT.

Because he is very, very, very Jewish, which I respect so much, he's basically in Jewish jail from Friday through Saturday night—house arrest, okay, but actually much worse because he and my Ivanka aren't allowed to have fun *or* work, no TV, no movies, no phone, no Internet, no driving, nothing. People in Secretary Ben Carson's Christian religion, Seventh-day Adventist, do the same thing; their holy day is Saturday, although they don't call it Sha-boom or whatever, like Judaism does. But it's not like there's ever going to be some Housing and Urban Development emergency where I'll need Ben on a Saturday, right? (Also, he's not strict about it, because when he was running against me, he definitely campaigned on Saturdays, which I could've hit him for at the time, but didn't.)

The Sunday shows had footage of the protesters and lawyers at the airports all trying to stop us from keeping America safe. "I wonder how much your buddy Soros is paying them?" I asked.

Jared just smiled. "Come on, tell me, I won't tweet it." Jared has a huge line of credit from George Soros for his real estate business. Like a *billion* dollars. We kept the story from getting out before the election, and I worried it would be a big problem for us with the conservatives, the Alex Jones folks, when it did break, which it just did, but Bannon says he'll make sure it "stays on the down-low in our zone." Steve is very tough. He reminds me of a tubby Roy Cohn, not gay but tough and funny like Roy except with more real, you know, *beliefs* and so forth. I know Steve looks like he has cancer or something, but I had people check it out and that's just the way he looks.

Somebody who'd been around the day before — Cohen or Eisenberg, one of the young national security guys who are allowed to work all weekend even though they're Jewish — told me not to worry about the protesters. Because Americans don't care for the pro-Muslim protesters, which is true. But also because, which I didn't know, by using some kind of high-tech radar we can clock in to all the protesters' phones, so it's like they're registering with us, then keep the numbers on file in case any of them turn out to be terrorists or terrorist supporters or illegals. So what *looks* bad for us, people don't realize, is actually a *win*. Which, quite frankly, has always been a big part of my success in business. Marketing 101.

"You saw what McCain and Graham said?" Jared asked. "Criticizing the executive order, the rollout?"

"Already have a response. Here's how I'm hitting them: 'WARNING: John McCain & never-married "Lindsey" Graham, major losers, planning to start World War III — soon! Not my fault when they do! Scary!'"

Jared shot me this really annoying look of his, like I'm his son. But I handed him the phone. Especially since he's not getting directly paid, sometimes I have to let him be "Senior White House Adviser." It's why I let him have his own little intelligence briefing every morning. Better than listening to him go on and on about my presidency being "in beta" with "limited-time windows of opportunity to move the needle," and how I have "core competencies in disruption" but I need to "get buy-in" if I want to "take Washington to the next level."

He changed my tweet, made it:

"Senators and former pres candidates McCain & Graham should focus energies on ISIS, immigration & border security, not premature criticism."

"Come on, *Professor Kushner*—'premature criticism'? That's like 'erectile dysfunction.' So off-brand, so not Trump! Boring, boring, boring. Plus, I'm definitely putting World War III back in." Which I did, and punched "Tweet," *boom*. I am the president. Jared went down to do some work in his office in the West Wing.

He hasn't called me *Mr. President* yet.

My daughter does sometimes, but it's more humorous, like with a fun wink, the way Marilyn Monroe sang it to President Kennedy. Which by the way isn't "inappropriate" of me to say—Va-va-va-vanka said it herself. She also told me Marilyn was almost exactly her age at the time of the "Happy Birthday, Mr. President" show at the Garden, and that she killed herself like two months afterward. Sad.

Why is there nothing good at all on TV on Sundays after the news shows? It was true when I was a kid and what, twenty-five years later, with a million channels, it's still true. I want to put forward a plan to fix that, and have already asked my great new FCC chairman to take care of it—Ajit Pai, Indian guy, great young guy, Harvard, *Ajit Pai*, I love saying Ajit's name, fantastic name. On the other hand, the lack of good TV in America on weekend afternoons, I must say, is a big reason I took up golf in the first place, and why I've won *eighteen* club championships so far. And therefore also why I now own the finest golf properties in the world, the greatest collection in history. So out of bad can sometimes come good. And as president, because they'll try to keep me from golfing every weekend, the lack of good TV will give me time to write this book, by talking, as I'm doing now, here in the Treaty Room. Which really may be my favorite room in the White House—only I come here, extremely comfortable sofa, concealed minifridge for the Diet Cokes, credenza for the Doritos and Lays and chocolate-covered pretzels I have flown in from Pittsburgh, a really fantastic gold mirror, very old, plus a nice balcony and a decent view. And the only large-screen TV they had in the place, if you can believe it, in 2017.

As a result of the TV situation on the weekends that I don't golf, Ivanka says I get "moody." Which is why she told her friend Wendi Murdoch to tell Rupert to try to make more of his calls to me on Sundays or, even better, Saturdays, when she has to be so Jewish all day long. That's also why they scheduled our first White House movie for today in the screening room in the East Wing. (What is with all the bright red fabric in there? Like a strip club.) It's *Finding Dory*, the computer cartoon about the fish. Ivanka's bringing over the kids, and it had the most successful opening weekend of any cartoon ever, grossed a billion dollars, so I—

What the hell? Uh-oh! Landline ringing on the Treaty Desk!

> *VOICE MEMO: Presidential to-do list*
> *Song, "WHAT THE HELL / UH-OH / LANDLINE*
> *RINGING ON THE TREATY DESK," © 2017 by*
> *Donald J. Trump.*

The call was from Mad Dog and Mike Flynn. SEAL Team Six did a commando raid against al-Qaeda in Yemen, which is the little one at the bottom of Saudi Arabia.

"Around forty-five dead, Mr. President," Flynn said.

"*Fantastic*," I said. "Forty-five down, how many to go?"

Mad Dog said it wasn't that simple, because about thirty were civilians, only fourteen definite al-Qaeda. (I'm not quoting him directly because he said he might have to resign if I did that. Fine. I've made a similar deal with my wife, the First Lady.)

"Okay, Mad Dog," I said, "but fourteen is still good. Why don't you guys sound happier? Yemen is on our list, right, one of the bad Arab countries, where we're vetting all the terrorist immigrants? Well, this shows people that a lot of the Yemenians *are* terrorists, and we're whacking them there so they don't come here and destroy America! You can't say that but I can. I'll tweet it. And we'll get *Fox & Friends* to do a split screen in the morning—like on the right they show some of the ones in the garb at JFK, and on the left a few of the dead ones in Yemen. Pictures worth thousands of words! You with me, Mad Dog? Mike?" It was Marketing 101 blended with Leadership 101.

Mad Dog told me that the bad Arab hombres got one of our SEALs, that even with months of planning things sometimes go wrong, and would I please stop calling him Mad Dog.

Jared came upstairs and I gave him the lowdown.

"Wow," he said. "That's too bad. Really sad."

We sat for a minute, the two of us. It was a moment of silence. Not complete silence, because the TV was still on, the afternoon rerun of *Meet the Press* with Chuck Todd, who is practically bald now, which I guess is why he grew that ridiculous, disgusting goatee. And I was checking Twitter—somebody points out that the ACLU and ISIS both have four letters and two of them are vowels. Interesting. Nothing yet about Yemen.

"You know," I finally said to Jared, "the media will blame me for the SEAL getting killed. And the civilians. If they really were civilians. Mad Dog said it was a mission they'd planned for months, meaning under Obama, right? I *guess* I gave the thumbs-up last week sometime, but it's the generals who call the shots, not me, that was always the Trump platform. I didn't write the courses for Trump University, I don't tell the guys with the bull-dozer how to put the sand in the bunkers or water in the hazards. Right? I mean, Mad Dog and my other generals are extremely well respected, the most respected that we've had since Patton, so I trusted them. That's what you do, as the commander in chief."

"Uh-huh," Jared said.

One of the servants, a steward, was at the door with my Oval-tine and Sunday breakfast fries and Jared's carrots and tea. "Hey, Rodrigo, come on in, what's shaking?" Rodrigo is my favorite White House servant, not one of the navy "sailors" who I feel like are being punished doing this kind of work. Rodrigo is cheerful, very respectful, like I'm the king. The other day he told me a Philippines proverb, "*Bagong hari, bagong ugali*," which at first I thought was some kind of dirty joke, but he told me it means "New king, new character," meaning I'm the new king and I'll do it my way. I choked up when he showed me the picture on his phone of his cousin giving the finger in front of the new seventy-five-story Trump Tower Manila, tallest building in the Philippines.

"Jared, try a fry, they actually make a very decent fry here." He passed, *of course*. "Rodrigo, did I tell you the final Miss Universe

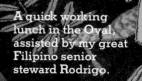

A quick working lunch in the Oval, assisted by my great Filipino senior steward Rodrigo.

62

I owned was Miss Philippines?"

"Yes, Mr. President, you did."

"Actually, I owned her as Miss Philippines, but by the time she became Miss Universe I'd sold the business for an incredible amount of money to Rahm Emanuel's brother. You were here when Rahm was chief of staff?"

"Yes, Mr. President."

"How do you think Reince is doing, Rodrigo?"

"Excuse me, Mr. President?"

"As chief of staff—is he doing it okay? The way he scurries around doesn't strike you as . . . whatever?"

"Mr. Priebus seems on the ball, sir."

"Okay. Anyhow, at that 2015 pageant, the first one I didn't own, remember how they completely screwed it up and gave the crown to the wrong girl, Miss Colombia, before they realized your girl won?" He said he'd heard about it and also told me Joe Scarborough and Mika Brezhnev were here for lunch downstairs in the Blue Room.

"Right. You know," I said, "she was the third Miss Philippines to become Miss Universe. Very light, German dad, but still counted as a minority."

I always compliment Joe on his hair, which truly is excellent hair, very impressive hair, like mine, and I also commented very favorably on his height, because he's as tall as I am, great height. But when I asked how he thought my first week as president had gone, he goes "Not so well." He's eating with me and my family in the White House on Day . . . Seven or . . . Day Ten, I tell him his hair is beautiful, and he has to be rude? Unbelievable. But instead of telling him "Fuck you, Joe, get the fuck out of here," pardon my French, I was very presidential and took it as a joke, reminding everybody he was busting my balls to pretend like he was an independent "journalist." And in fact, when he told us he and Mika were getting married, and Jared offered to do the cere-mony for them with his fake license he used for Eric's wedding at Mar-a-Lago, I was *so* presidential, I said, "*You*, Jared? Why *you*? When they could have the president of the United States do it?"

★ ★ ★ ★ ★ ★ ★ ★ ★

I'M THE PRESIDENT

W ow: That was a whole chapter but I only got through one long weekend. Important weekend for sure, America already becoming great again. But I realize I have to pick up the pace if this book isn't going to turn into one of those crazy thousand-page Bill Clinton cinder blocks. New rule: At least one whole week per chapter, unless I start a war in Syria or North Korea.

Kidding! Nobody can take a joke anymore.

I expected the so-called federal judges to rule in favor of allowing evil into America. I expected a fight. I love a fight. Ask the guys on Midland Parkway in Queens if I didn't make them regret calling me Ronald Richie Rich Rump—one kid with very permanent regrets. Ask certain people in the gaming and banking industries if I'm not a tough, tough fighter when I need to be. I love the fight, but I didn't have an attorney general yet, which tied one hand behind my back and was also very unfair to my little pixie

Jeffy Sessions. But at least I have my White House counsel, Don McGahn, a very tough Irishman whose uncle Paddy was my Atlantic City casino lawyer for years.

And unlike the attorney general, McGahn is *my* lawyer, which is beautiful—he's right upstairs in the West Wing, I get the attorney-client privilege, *and* I don't pay his bills, which would be like a million bucks a year. Like this fantastic financial guy Anthony Scaramucci I'm trying to hire, he reminds me a little of myself, great education and good-looking and has some money but a regular guy, plus really great hair. And since McGahn's name is *Don*, talking to him is kind of like I'm talking to myself, which is good. He came into the Oval Office to tell me that, so far, they'd sued us in New York City, San Francisco, and Seattle.

"Not San Diego yet, Don? I hope San Diego, I really do. You know why, Don? Because that judge who extorted me for twenty-five million in the Trump University case, the Mexican, is in San Diego. If he ruled against us on the terrorist immigrants, it'd prove he was unfair to us because the Wall will keep out his cousins."

"We've got a problem with the acting attorney general," Don told me. "She won't defend us in court."

"The same Obama lady who came over here last week trying to get me to fire Mike Flynn? Wow, power's really gone to her head after ten days on the job."

"Actually, Yates has been at Justice for twenty-seven years, Mr. President."

"Oh, so she's civil service, phoning it in, timeserver, happy earning 200K. I'll call and fire her personally. By the way, Don, isn't insubordination a *crime* when we're talking national security? I think it is." Trump delegates, but Trump is also hands-on when it counts. And if I called her, I'd get to say *"You're fired!"* for the first time as president. People around the world are literally holding their breaths waiting for that moment. I had my cell phone recorder on, as I do a lot now, and put the landline on speaker because I definitely wanted this on tape. Exciting! "Okay, tell the girl out there to phone Justice."

He said I really shouldn't call her. Okay, *fine*. But then I had the idea of farming out the firing to our little White House HR guy, whose name I don't even remember, which I knew would be a perfect you-know-what to the you-know-what on her way out, pardon my French. But also, I said, make it a letter, hand-delivered right away—cold but classy, also a great scene when she reads it and then chokes up, maybe drops the letter to the floor and stumbles a little as she puts her hands to her face and starts to cry.

I also personally quarterbacked the press release. I dictated while Hope Hicks, my great and very beautiful young director of strategic communications, did the writing with a pen by hand, which I love. "Okay," I said, "'the, quote, acting, unquote, quote, attorney general, unquote, who is very, very weak on borders and also very, very weak on illegal immigration, has betrayed her employers, President Trump and the American people, in a totally disloyal way.'" I agreed with Don and Hope that we could take out "disloyal" because it means the same as "betray," but that we *definitely* had to keep "weak" and at least one "very." So we did. I'm the president.

I must tell you, at that moment, coming off such a tough weekend, the protests and the legal fighting, the no golf, I was finally feeling great again. Which is better for America than if the president doesn't feel great. I was on a roll. After I hit somebody who hit me, I like to be nice to somebody who was nice to me, so I decided to call Judge Gorsuch and tell him he won the Supreme Court seat, even though I didn't have my little sheet about him. Trump can wing it. Leadership 101.

"Hey, Judge Gorsuch. Whoops, I mean, *Justice* Gorsuch of the United States Supreme Court—you're *hired*!" He lives out in the Rocky Mountains, so I sang the first line of "Rocky Mountain High."

He chuckled. "Thank you so much, Mr. President. I'm deeply grateful and honored."

"Hey, look, I see your area code is 303—here it's 202. Spooky, right?"

Reince ran into the Oval, looking even more nervous than usual.

"Hey, Neil," I said, "you beat out twenty great guys for this job! And I'm including the women, too, three or four of them in there. And several minorities, which people say actually made it harder for a guy like you. The same way I beat out seventeen people to get the nomination, you know, all these governors and senators, and Dr. Ben Carson, I beat all of them. And the twenty running against *you* weren't buying ads saying these horrible, horrible, untrue, unfair things about you on TV, right? And then I beat *eighteen*, counting Hillary. I won't ask you who you voted for, Judge."

"I appreciate that, Mr. President."

"But *me*, right, Neil?"

He chuckled.

"Just kidding," I said. "The sarcasm."

He chuckled again. I was building a relationship with a guy I needed to be on my side for the full four or eight years—because it turns out not even a president can fire these guys, even the ones they hired.

"Ha ha ha," I laughed. "Although I do know you're a good conservative Republican, so, seriously, I'm assuming you were one of my Colorado voters, even though we supposedly lost Colorado, and we'll leave it there. Because *Hillary*—I don't think so, am I right? Not a guy who supports the Constitution as strongly as you do and hates abortion so much. And she gives lawyers such a bad name. Funny story: The First Lady, she's Slovenian, when she was my fiancée and I told her my *lawyer* needed her to sign a prenup, she got confused—she didn't get the difference between the words 'lawyer' and 'liar.' And I know Mrs. Gorsuch is from, um . . . ?"

Don McGahn lifted a book with what looked to me like a Confederate flag on the cover.

"—from the South. I was married to a girl from the South, didn't work out, but great people. I did so well in the South last November, so amazingly well all over the South, as you probably know, fifty-point margins."

Don was now shaking his head and pointing to my bust of Churchill.

"Although I know Mrs. Gorsuch is English, of course, the South of England, right, where London is, which, over there, they do call 'the South.' My mother was Scottish. People say I'm against foreigners, but three of my four grandparents were foreigners and two of my wives! By the way, I knew Princess Di, dated her briefly, beautiful girl, fantastic skin, so sad. And Mrs. Gorsuch is also, I understand, a very accomplished . . . you know . . ."

Now Reince was sitting up very straight in his chair with his hands on his lap, bouncing his head and upper body.

"—*lady*, a really *attractive* lady, where it counts, at night, making you feel like a man. Which is so important." Now Reince looked like he was going to cry; I found out later she was a big equestrian. But I'm telling you this because it's a fantastic example of one of the reasons I've been so successful—I'm very quick, improvise, keep the ball in the air, don't let things throw me.

"But you know, Neil—can I call you Neil, Neil?—in addition to being so conservative and so smart, Columbia, Harvard . . . we love the Ivy League, don't we? I'm Wharton, University of Pennsylvania. I also like that you've been a Catholic *and* a Protestant, and then went with Protestant. I'm Protestant, too. Because, no offense to anybody, *confession*? I don't think so. Not without my lawyer present. Kidding. But it's also great that you're a *young* man, Neil, almost the youngest on my list, which is so important for the Supreme Court. And quite frankly you *look* great, too, not just the white hair, distinguished, like Mike Pence, but Neil, you're a very good-looking guy, much more than any of the others. Central casting! Also, I must tell you, *great voice*—like an old-fashioned announcer."

"I appreciate that, sir."

"You could be a broadcaster, I'm serious, it's one of the best voices in our whole Administration. And Gorsuch, that's German, which I also love—I'm German, love the Germans."

"Actually, Mr. President, as I disappointed you before, when we met, Gorsuch is actually the English side of my family."

"Nope, sorry, that's definitely German. One last thing, Neil, on these so-called judges in Seattle and wherever ruling against us on the Middle East travel rules—you probably know the guys? And as of tomorrow you'll be the ultimate superstar to them, right? Well, maybe you could make a few calls, tell these guys it would be very, very meaningful to you personally if they made the correct decisions on this deal—probably just say 'correct,' and leave it at that."

But traditions, protocols, rule of law, he said, blah-blah-blah. "Right, I totally understand," I said. "I *respect* your answer *very much*." I realized he probably figured we were taping him. Smart.

An hour later, I was upstairs in the main house, out of the suit, bare feet, Coke, Doritos, "*Hannity* and chill," as Ivanka says, wondering if it'd be okay to ask Rodrigo to clip the big toenails—and I suddenly see the gossip all over Twitter: Gorsuch, Gorsuch, Gorsuch. I had Reince and Hope come back. Then Bannon and Kellyanne showed up, and before long Jared was also there. It's amazing the way they do that: You order one, you get the whole set. It's like *Our Gang*. (That's what I said at a meeting

I SAW BANNON AND KELLYANNE AND JARED STANDING NEAR BEN CARSON: "HEY, LOOK— IT'S SPANKY AND DARLA AND ALFALFA AND BUCKWHEAT!"

last week when I saw Bannon and Kellyanne and Jared standing near Ben Carson: "Hey, look—it's Spanky and Darla and Alfalfa *and* Buckwheat!" Everyone laughed, especially Ben.)

"We're losing control of the Supreme Court finale," I told them when they all got to the Oval. "If everyone knows ahead of time Gorsuch is the winner, it'll kill our ratings tomorrow. Trust me."

Nobody had any idea what to do. It was up to me.

"So, the runner-up, the one we dinged because he was a little too nice to the Central American illegals . . . ?"

"Judge Hardiman," Don said.

Working with Rodrigo,
my senior steward and special
liaison for East Asian labor
issues, at Mar-a-Lago,
the Southern White House,
which I own.

"Right, Hardiman. By the way? I felt sorry for him—that *name*, you know they busted his balls growing up, Hardy Boy, Har-Har-Har-Man, Hard-On. But he's in Pittsburgh, right, that's like a five-hour drive?"

"Mr. President," Don McGahn said, "you want Judge Hardiman to drive to Washington to find out he's not being nominated?"

"No! Not all the way. Kellyanne and Sean will let the reporters all *think* he's still in the running, they set up outside his house tomorrow morning, he comes out and drives east for like an hour, has lunch, whatever, as a favor to me. But the media *thinks* he's on his way to D.C. for a final meeting with me and a showdown with Gorsuch. They think, 'Oh my God, Trump is turning this into *Celebrity Apprentice*.' Like in Season 7, where it came down to Piers Morgan and Trace Adkins and Piers won. By the way, it was so great when Trace came back in Season 13 and *did* win. So maybe when the old lady finally gives up the ghost, Ginsburg, we give hers to Judge Hard-On."

★ ★

A VERY RELIABLE SOURCE told me NBC still holds a tremendous grudge against Trump for ruining their profits after I pulled out of *The Apprentice*, so in retaliation they ordered Joe Scarborough to betray and attack me. I phoned Joe this morning to give him another chance to do the right thing, to be a real conservative, like Hannity. But he was very rude—rude not just to Donald Trump but to the *president* and the *presidency*. By the way, back when they started MSNBC I thought that name was so weird, but recently somebody explained to me that's how you know they always planned to flip it totally into Democrat fake news—*Ms*. NBC. Amazing.

★ ★ ★ ★ ★ ★ ★ ★ ★ ★ ★ ★ ★ ★ ★ ★ ★ ★ ★ ★

THE CEREMONY where I announced Gorsuch was fantastic, here in the White House in the double-height room with the columns and chandeliers—Rodrigo says a lot of the staff has already started calling it Trump Hall. "Wow," I told him, "that's amazing, because at the Southern White House, we have the official Donald J. Trump Ballroom, completely gold." I was great, literally everyone said so, and I heard some people say Gorsuch and I standing together almost looked like twins, except for his white hair, now that I'm back to my fighting weight, lost the pounds I put on during the campaign. A lot of people said Gorsuch did very well, too.

Right after the ceremony I was headed upstairs when my chief of staff and chief strategist pulled me aside—Reince looked upset but Bannon was smiling.

"Public transit guard in Denver just got shot and killed," Reince said. "By a Muslim extremist."

"Sad. But a total birdie or eagle travel-ban-wise, right?" Bannon was nodding. "Reince, have you called Kellyanne and Sean? It's like when San Bernardino happened a month before the first primaries. That's when my political brand really got hot. Where's he from, the terrorist?"

"American," Reince said, "native born, Texas."

"Yeah," Bannon said, "but 'Joshua Cummings'? I guess he might be a white guy."

I definitely didn't chuckle. "But all his Muslim friends," I said, "were aware he was bad news but didn't say anything, right?" These Muslims are like teamsters. It's sad.

Reince was reading off his phone. "Actually, his mosque had reported him to Homeland Security. And here's a photo—the guy's white. It won't get any coverage."

"You win some, you lose some," I said. By which I meant that, while I was deeply saddened by the murder of an American in uniform by *a radical Islamic terrorist*, the commander in chief must always play through the pain. At least it was only one victim, not like under Obama, when practically every terrorist killed a hundred innocent people.

Reince held up his phone to show us the CNN headline about my Gorsuch ceremony—"Trump puts on a flawless show." Flawless. CNN said *flawless*. In other words, it occurred to me when I thought about it later, I was impeccable, unblemished, unimpaired, unsullied, faultless, irreproachable, and perfect. On Day Nine or Day Twelve or whatever, everyone was already admitting the Trump Administration was *perfect*.

★ ★ ★ ★ ★ ★ ★ ★ ★

I FEEL LIKE A NEW MAN

N ever forget the important life lesson I mentioned earlier—how the ups don't last long. There's always something—as my dad used to say, a fly in the ointment, a skunk at the picnic, a turd in the punch bowl, an African American in the woodpile, some unauthorized foreign tenant hiding in the attic. He was a loyalty guy, my dad, and I'm a loyalty guy. So right after I gave Gorsuch one of the greatest jobs in America—only $244,000, but no mandatory retirement—so times forty years that's $10 million—plus book money, speech money, probably endorsement money, summers completely off—the guy comes back to Washington, at our expense, and starts telling senators he finds my criticism of judges who let terrorists into America "disheartening" and "demoralizing." Could you believe that? He even did it on the same day the judges at the worst appeals court went against us—judges out west, where he's from, by the way. I was very, very disappointed. Majorly disappointed. In fact, I went back to our vetting file on Neil and thought about putting a certain very interesting item into a tweet.

But then I decided against it. Because I'm a nice guy, and Justice Gorsuch is our guy, and I wanted the win for America. Although now he knows I know about that interesting item from 1988. So we're good, I'm sure we're good.

★ ★ ★ ★ ★ ★ ★ ★ ★ ★ ★ ★ ★ ★ ★ ★ ★ ★ ★

KELLYANNE SAYS that since I'd spent two entire weeks as president, all at the White House, it was okay to head down to Florida for the weekend. Headed there now. I'm in Air Force One's Oval Office. Which is tight, and not an oval, but at least it now has a new large-screen TV with a fantastic remote control, state of the art. Soon I'll be at my Mar-a-Lago, getting the tan back up where it belongs, surrounded by my hundreds of longtime loyal members, all my longtime loyal employees—although I'm going to have Rodrigo start flying back and forth, to be a steward at *both* White Houses, the old one and the fantastic Southern one. With his Philippines background, it seems like he'd be a perfect fit down there, with the palm trees and the ocean and the Spanish and the heat, and all the constant lawn care.

And tomorrow, instead of sitting down to some meeting at 9 a.m., with everybody trying to show how serious and smart they are, I'll be teeing off at Trump International Golf Club, which has twenty-seven holes, no two alike and the highest elevation of any course in the State of Florida, a fantastic course, where I've won the club championship three times so far. I *own* the club, which is only twenty minutes away from the Southern White House, which I also own. Which I mention because it means that, in addition to being a perfect place for any American to hold weddings and corporate meetings and experience the Trump lifestyle, Trump *International* will be a perfect venue for making great trade and world peace deals with visiting world leaders—deals that benefit you, the forgotten Americans. Win-win-win.

Also, I'm very much looking forward to spending the weekend with my beautiful wife and our top-notch son for the first time in weeks, which will be great, since I miss them both very much, of course. The First Lady has not been to the White House since the inauguration, partly because she has been working hard preparing a new lawsuit against the terrible English newspaper that printed horrible, vicious, disgusting, very untrue lies about how she earned her living when she was younger—lies that have harmed her unique, once-in-a-lifetime opportunity, as an extremely famous and well-known person, to launch a broad-based commercial brand in multiple product categories, including apparel, shoes, jewelry, timepieces, cosmetics, hair and skin care, fragrance, body scrubs and muds, financial services, dairy substitutes, antifungals, major appliances, auto repair, and sandwich bags, each of which could have garnered multimillion-dollar business relationships for a multiyear term in which she will be one of the most photographed women in the world. But despite all of that, as well as her time-consuming primary custodial responsibility for our fantastic son, my wife will be joining me at the White House for a great event in eleven days, as First Lady. After that, she'll probably spend at least one night at the Executive Mansion every nine to eleven days through the first and second quarters, as the mood strikes her.

Saturday I got to spend five hours on the course. Turns out, when you're president, the trip from Mar-a-Lago across the bridge on Southern Boulevard to Trump International is only *fifteen* minutes. Shot a sixty-seven, five under par, which I must honestly tell you is an incredible score, an unbelievable score. I feel like a new man. "You mean 'incredible' and 'unbelievable' like 'not true'?" my youngest son asked when I got home to Mar-a-Lago. He wasn't smiling, so I don't think he was making fun of me.

★ ★ ★ ★ ★ ★ ★ ★ ★

I LIKE TOUGH

Because the First Lady can't be in Washington as much as she and I would very much like, I often have Ivanka and Jared join me for dinner at the White House. Tonight I surprised them with some special kosher steak.

"Is that the greatest steak you've ever eaten? Walking around in Nebraska this morning, all koshered up by the afternoon, on White House china tonight," I said. "Air Force is flying them in for me from the base in Omaha to Andrews on one of their C-17 Globemasters. Globemasters!"

"*Ooh*, ultimate farm to table!" Ivanka said.

Her oohs are like the First Lady did when she was young, very cute, very sexy. "Hold on a second, baby."

> *VOICE MEMO: Presidential to-do list*
> *Song, "NEBRASKA THIS MORNING / KOSHERED*
> *UP THIS AFTERNOON / ON WHITE HOUSE CHINA*
> *TONIGHT," Toby Keith! © 2017 by Donald J. Trump.*

They smiled. But I'm serious about the songs.

"Wouldn't it be fantastic if the Air Force could also supply some of the same meat to Trump International down the street? We already know the steak business, right? But super limited edition! Not necessarily kosher. Trump Globemaster Same-Day Steaks! Plus, a new revenue center for the Pentagon."

Now they chuckled. That's a problem being president—for *me*. With a lot of my ideas, everybody now thinks I'm joking. But I'm usually not. And sometimes I think *they're* joking when it turns out they're not—like when somebody mentioned "Gurbanguly Berdimuhamedow, the president of Turkmenistan," I laughed out loud and said "*Shhhh!*" because I thought the PC police would call it "racist." (The guy is real, and so is Turkmenistan.) But whenever I tell them *I'm* not joking, they give me weird looks—or glance at each other when they think I'm looking down at my phone, like Jared did at dinner tonight when I dictated the memo about my latest song.

"You know what I mean, Dad?" Ivanka had changed the subject.

"Where the *hell* are you going with *that*, Vanky-panky?" She'd said this weird thing about Steve Bannon. She said he reminds her of my second wife, her first stepmother. Like Marla, she said, Steve is a flirt and a Southerner who looked really good when he was young and never quite made it in show business. And like with Marla, I'd had what Ivanka called "a long-term man crush" on Steve, which doesn't mean gay, before I officially dumped his predecessors and got together with him.

"Steve's a hundred times smarter than Marla," I said. "I think his IQ is like 200, 225, math *and* verbal. And Marla doesn't drink, unlike certain White House advisers and ex-wives I could mention."

But that led Ivanka and Jared and me into a very honest discussion about Steve Bannon. Who, by the way, is now getting even *more* coverage from the media since I put him on my National Security Council with the special platinum all-access VIP pass. (*Finally* he stopped with the "served aboard the USS *Foster* in the Pacific in the Cold War" stuff.) I signed the order for that, by the way, on the Saturday of that tough weekend right in the middle of all the disgusting airport chaos that Steve and his team didn't foresee, when Jared was unavailable because he so strictly observes Shebang or Schmata or whatever. According to Jared's "analytics," Steve has already gotten as much coverage as Karl Rove got during Bush's whole first year, more than any senior White House strategist in history. Food for thought. By the way, Bannon's office in the West Wing is right next to Jared's, and the walls in the West Wing, except for special ones in the Oval and the Situation Room, are not so thick.

Which reminded me. "Vanky," I told her, "good news—I gave Reince the official go-ahead—you're getting that West Wing office you wanted, right upstairs. Happy Valentine's Day."

"*Ooh, thanks*," she said, and blew me a kiss. I caught it and put it in my mouth. Nice.

Rodrigo came in to clear our plates. "Don't let all that fantastic steak these two gym rats didn't eat go to waste—take it home! Maybe give some to my boy Anthony, too, if he's still standing guard out there—if he hasn't *retired* yet!"

Anthony is young, but I found out that he and a hundred other of the Secret Service African Americans just got paid off like a quarter million apiece in a settlement for "discrimination" by past administrations—not by us, by others, including Bill Clinton's, which the media has never written about. Who signed that $24 million check on his way out? *Obama*, of course. I asked Anthony if he's got his eye on one of the top-of-the-line Cadillac Escalades, because a friend of mine in Miami, Ed something, major Trump supporter, is the second-largest Cadillac dealer in America, so I could get him a beautiful deal. Anthony told me he prefers German cars. I bet Obama drives an Audi, too. Not many people realize an agent like Anthony makes $142,000 base, $160,000 with overtime. Seriously! As much as a general! Almost as much as a senator! Wow. I mean, good for Anthony and all the lucky African Americans in America. But wow.

All the media focus on Bannon is another part of the Trump Bump. I get that. But the headline on the *New York Times* editorial—"President Bannon"? Two days later, the Bannon *cover* story on *Time*. Two days after that, *Saturday Night Live*'s skit—with Bannon treating Trump like a retarded boy—so offensive. Then this cartoon on Colbert's *Late Show* tonight, where I'm crying and Bannon is tucking me into bed. So disrespectful, so unpatriotic, so vicious.

But Steve is another tough Irishman. I like tough. Mike Flynn is Irish, also tough, although that kind of Irish wiry tough that can suddenly flip over to crazy wild man. Sean Spicer is Irish, tough in the way youngest kids in Irish families are, the chubby ones who get razzed and beat up a lot. Kellyanne is Irish, also very tough. She turned fifty on Inauguration Day. *Phenomenal* body on Kellyanne, if I'm being perfectly honest. And *four kids* came out of there, practically last month, she has *young* kids. People call Kellyanne a butterface, which is very unkind, and come on, guys, the lady is *fifty* years old—which by the way my wife will be during my first term, as Ivanka reminded me again, said we should plan a big fiftieth birthday celebration. The First Lady was twenty-eight when we met. She said then that I was like this certain god in ancient Slovenia, in their religion or whatever, who has tons of gold and a gun that never misses and a magic fiddle that makes everyone dance. That was so hot when she said that. Wow. Time flies.

But back to toughness, which I love, even in women, to a certain extent. Reince is a good guy, polite, intelligent, sweet guy, trying to do his best, but he's not what you'd call a tough guy. The same with Sean—nice, follows orders, works like hell to survive, not a *loser*, like I've heard people say, but not your Mr. Toughie, either. Ivanka is very tough—in fact, she's like a secretly tougher version of me because she can *act nice* much better than I can, *so* nice, *so* sweet, so feminine, so liberal, whatever, and then *boom*, you're dead. Jared is similar—he was so polite to Chris Christie for so long before he pulled the trigger on him, like a coldhearted hit man. But then the Jewish people tend to be tough people, even the ones born into money. Such as Jared's dad, very tough son of a gun who Chris Christie sent to a prison in Alabama for blackmailing a snitch, a snitch who happened to be his brother-in-law, by setting the guy up with a hooker. I won't go into the details, but they're really amazing. It was a sad time for Jared.

> **IVANKA IS VERY TOUGH—IN FACT, SHE'S LIKE A SECRETLY TOUGHER VERSION OF ME BECAUSE SHE CAN *ACT NICE* MUCH BETTER THAN I CAN, *SO* NICE, *SO* SWEET, SO FEMININE, SO LIBERAL, WHATEVER, AND THEN *BOOM*, YOU'RE DEAD.**

A lot of time in families, the tough and weak come in sets. For instance, I'm tough, and my sister the brilliant federal judge is tough, but my two brothers—the one who was supposed to take over the business from my dad and the one who raises horses or whatever—not really tough guys. And the family toughness sets can come in threes, too, like with my children from my first marriage — Ivanka (spicy), Don Junior (medium), and Eric (mild), or like the three Kennedy brothers, JFK and Bobby and Teddy, although with them everyone finally respected the also-ran because he lived so long. It's all about harmony and balance, Ivanka says. I guess.

Nothing says fit and healthy like a good tan, and crucial to the Trump brand—so when I'm stuck in Washington with no time for golf, touch-ups are essential.

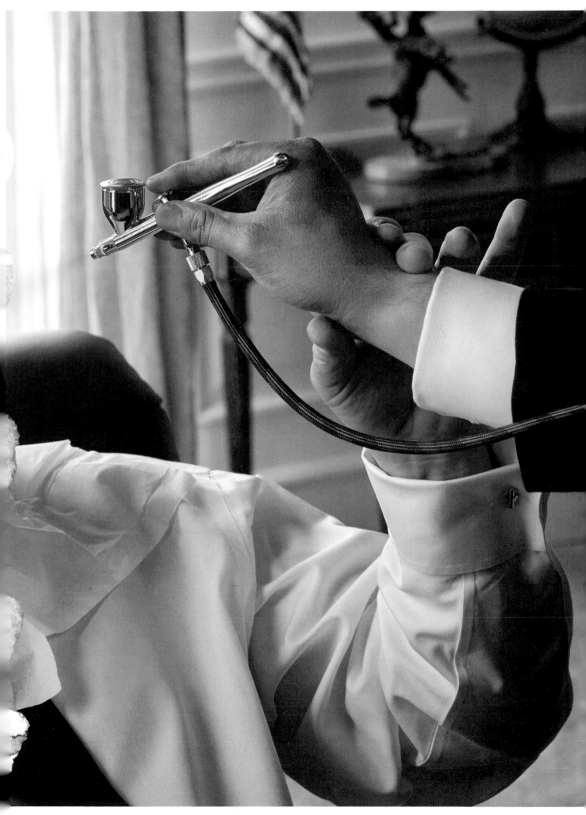

★ ★ ★ ★ ★ ★ ★ ★ ★

IT WAS ABOUT TO GET EVEN BETTER

The Japanese prime minister had been visiting for twenty-four hours, but this was my first real private time with him.

"Shinzō," I said, "what do you think of Reince Priebus?"

We were walking off the green of the first hole (fifteen-foot birdie for me, par four for him) at the beautiful Trump National Golf Club in Jupiter, Florida, about a half hour up the coast from the Southern White House.

I guess Prime Minister Abe didn't understand my question.

"My *Chief. Of. Staff*," I explained. The translator translated— although with that you never really know for sure, do you? "At the White House yesterday," I said, "short guy, dark hair, balding, looks a little Japanese come to think of it, always darting around. Reince Priebus? Good man, you think?"

Mr. Abe still looked confused, the way he had the night before, when I told him my dad was German, actually conceived *in Germany*, so no hard feelings whatsoever about World War II. Somebody golfing with us said later that maybe he got a little weird about *Reince Priebus* because he thought I was trying to make a joke about his Japanese accent, how they pronounce the *R*s. Which I wasn't, although it was funny to think about. I was totally presidential all weekend, totally "dignified." For instance, as we golfed on Saturday morning, I didn't make one of those jokes guys do about the short distance from the first to the second hole and how tight and hard to get into the second hole is. Which the translator probably would've messed up anyhow.

Instead, we discussed important issues. Concerning trade, I told the prime minister a story. Even if he hadn't come to visit me at Trump Tower when I was president-elect, just a week after my landslide victory, I told him, and even if he hadn't gifted me then with a gold, top-of-the-line $4,000 Japanese-made driver, he probably still would have been my first visiting foreign leader as President Trump—but who knows? He smiled. He was inscrutable, like they are, but I was sure he got my point.

"Shinzō," I continued, "you must know people who own at Trump Waikiki, right? In Honolulu? No? Beautiful 463-unit condo and hotel right on the beach, the most famous beach in the world. *Most* of the owners are Japanese! Right there across the bay from Pearl Harbor, but again, no hard feelings! So I've always wondered why was it always impossible for The Trump Organization to get anything built in Tokyo? Trade barriers! By the way, I'm told that my daughter Tiffany drives a Prius. And also, I am *personally* paying for your greens fees today and your lodging and meals at the Mar-a-Lago Club last night and tonight. Personally! Complimentary! No conflict of interest! Friends!"

We had a wide-ranging discussion—how America now lets Japan buy our natural gas, how we pay for the huge base on Okinawa protecting them and keep their neighbors in North Korea from nuking them, how the Mar-a-Lago Club was bestowed with the coveted *Six Star* Diamond Award, the top award, beyond the normal "five stars," from the American Academy of Hospitality Sciences, which gives out the Oscars to hotels and restaurants.*

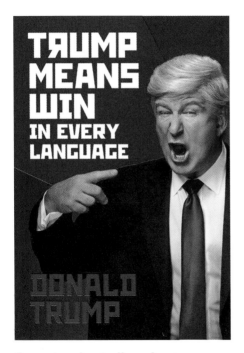

A previous bestseller—about my foreign policy negotiating skills.

By the end of the eighteen holes, Prime Minister Abe was very receptive and Japan and the United States had become, maybe, probably, closer allies than ever before in history. I shot a sixty-five, including a hole in one on Trump National's par-three fourteenth hole—which we didn't publicize, not even on Twitter. That round lifted our spirits so much that instead of heading straight back to the wives at Mar-a-Lago, we stopped to play another nine at Trump International in West Palm. (I did even better: thirty-two, four under par.) By the way, even though Rex Tillerson and nobody else from the State Department was with us that weekend, I was a perfect diplomat. For instance, I pronounced the prime minister's last name correctly every time, Ah-bay, not Abe like in Abe Lincoln, because I had the idea of thinking of it like *ah-so*, the Japanese word for "okay." By the way, I discuss many

*My youngest son just showed me how to insert the "footnotes." Wow! Computer genius. I wanted to say here that my other sons and I are such fans of the AAHS and its president and CEO, our friend and former *Miss Universe* judge Joey "No Socks" Cinque, that we've personally served on his board. Fantastic organization!

more tricks like that in my best-selling book on international business, *Trump Means Win in Every Language*.

My first twenty-four hours with a foreign leader as President Trump were already a gigantic success. And it was about to get even better.

At 7 p.m. at the Mar-a-Lago Club, what we call The Trump Golden Hour™ at all of our hotel and golf properties and my homes, I stepped onto the beautiful restaurant patio—and the entire crowd of ordinary Americans stood and applauded, Mar-a-Lago Club guests as well as Mar-a-Lago Club members, each dining on their individual choices from the multicultural cuisines—Continental, New World, Classical, and New Caribbean. Prime Minister Abe and his wife (and my wife, the First Lady) were very impressed by the standing ovation—and probably surprised, because of the dishonest media's coverage of Trump. You know how at Broadway shows, when the big star first appears on stage and the audience goes crazy and applauds, before he even does or says anything? It was just like that. And at the Mar-a-Lago Club, little did the audience know about the special, fantastic live show they were about to experience at no extra charge.

Right after we sat down to dinner (strip steak for me, fish for our Japanese friends, of course), a call came in on my presidential phone, the one that vibrates in a special, very intense way. It was the secretary of defense in Washington—just a few minutes earlier, he said North Korea had fired a missile . . . at *Japan*! I was seated right between Mr. and Mrs. Abe. Although neither of them speaks English well, if their country was being destroyed right now, I didn't want them to find out about it this way, by overhearing me talking to Mad Dog.

"Mad—*Jim*," I asked, "did the, you know . . . oreans-Kay uke-nay okyo-Tay?"

No! he said, practically screamed, in fact, it was just a *test launch* of a missile, fell into the ocean, no warhead.

"So we don't do anything, right? Fantastic. Whew."

I was relieved—my brilliant scientist uncle at MIT always told me that nuclear was so bad, the worst, we really don't want nuclear, even though we've always had the best nuclear— another one of those Cash-22s. But I also felt super excited because, after that, it became a fantastic scene from like *Fail-Safe* or *Deep Impact*, but adapted for live theater, starring me, Trump, as commander in chief, yet I could just enjoy the show. I told Prime Minister Abe the news, and then it was the two of us, the center of the action, the American leader and the obviously foreign leader, being briefed, looking at maps, nodding as translators said things. Our guys hustling around, moving chairs and candles, bringing out special digital flash-lights, saying "downrange" and "PACOM" and "carrier air wing." I loved hearing Abe call Flynn "Gen-ul-wah Fwin," but Mike was *so* excited it made me kind of sad. And it was a little much when Steve whispered to me, "Surface Warfare Officer Bannon, reporting for duty, *sir*," and he got so red-faced as the night wore on, I was afraid he might stroke out. Everybody in the restaurant was watching, and you could feel their excitement—because for all they knew, we were about to go into North Korea big-time! When I talked to Washington again, I got to use the Mar-a-Lago room they'd turned into a special high-tech bunker that jams all signals and beams and actually makes you invisible. When things on the patio were calming down, I asked my maître d' to have the piano guy start playing the *Mission: Impossible* music and the original James Bond theme song, which made the night even better. My little press conference with Abe at the end, and then it was a wrap, as we say in show business, totally presidential and outstanding.

Unfortunately, the media coverage was a complete and total lie. First of all: We avoided going to war with North Korea, right? Nobody mentioned that. Second of all, what do the pundits and reporters always say they *want*? Transparency! Openness! Like my incredibly popular free tweets, like my great interview of Romney at a fantastic public restaurant, like my press conferences that get the most viewers ever—the way I dealt with that alfresco North Korea crisis at Mar-a-Lago was the greatest display of transparency and openness in American foreign policy history, as many historians are saying.

Next morning, the prime minister passed on another round of golf at Trump International, which I understood, given his scores the day before (secret, but triple digit on the eighteen), so I reminded him to use the "grip tip" I'd given him. "And one last thing, Shinzō—what do you think of my national security adviser, General Flynn?"

He smiled and shrugged and made the three little circles with his finger around his ear. I gave him a thumbs-up and told him *the* vice president would definitely be in touch to work out the details on trade deals and so on. "Sayonara, Shinzō," I said, but then remembered you're only supposed to say that when it's good-bye forever, so I immediately added, "and we'll see each other again, meet you halfway next time, Trump Waikiki—my treat again!" As my dad always said about me, "At least the lying little bastard is fast on his feet," which my mom said he meant with love.

★ ★ ★ ★ ★ ★ ★ ★ ★ ★ ★ ★ ★ ★ ★ ★ ★ ★ ★ ★

FLYING BACK TO WASHINGTON, Bannon came into the mini Oval for a while, watched the news coverage of me being the most important world leader. As they talked on the show about Flynn and Russia, I was glad Mike had had so much fun being

Mr. Military at Mar-a-Lago, and I thought of *The Godfather*, the scene where Michael Corleone asks Tom Hagen, "Where does it say that you can't kill a cop?" Corleone tells him, "It's not personal. It's strictly business." And also the scene when Michael says Fredo has a good heart but he's weak and stupid and this is life and death.

I kind of think of Bannon as my Tom, the Robert Duvall character in *The Godfather*—a guy like me, like us, valuable guy, but not family. And then suddenly Steve did that mind-reading thing he does, which can be creepy. "Mr. President," he said, "I agree with Flynn about a lot of things, but he *is* weak and stupid and this *is* life and death and nobody says you can't fire a national security adviser after twenty-two days."

HE LOOKED SO MUCH LIKE FREDO RIGHT THEN. EVEN THOUGH I WASN'T ACTUALLY HAVING HIM "KILLED" AND HE HADN'T BETRAYED ME OR THE FAMILY. YET.

Mike always really, really enjoyed being Trump's buddy, my sidekick during the campaign, but as Jared and Ivanka point out, I'd only known him for like a year. "Mike," I told him the next day, "it's terrible what the fake media has done to you, the disgusting and I'm sure untrue stories about you and the Russians and the rest of it, but the Mike I can't fire"—that's what Bannon calls Pence—"says you lied to him about your chats with Sergey and so on. But I must tell you, Mike, you've been a major, major asset to me in the White House these last three weeks–plus, very major." He looked so much like Fredo right then. Even though I wasn't actually having him "killed" and he hadn't betrayed me or the family. Yet. I don't think. "I'll tweet about you, okay, I'll put out tremendously nice tweeting about you. As you know, I'm a big loyalty guy. The biggest."

In fact, I proved that the next morning, right after a briefing in the Oval when we prevented some serious terrorism—Mad Dog, General Kelly, Jeffy, *the* vice president and the FBI director, some others. As the meeting broke up, I asked the FBI director to stick around for a minute. I made him sit right in front of the official presidential desk. Management 101.

"*James*," I said when we were alone, very respectful, because I think he's probably one of these guys who can't stand it if you call him Jim, like the ones who insist on "Stephen" or "Gregory" instead of Steve or Greg, which always strikes me as a bit sissy. "So get the leakers, okay? We both hate the leakers, right? Get all the leakers, put them in jail, I'm counting on you, James. But with Mike Flynn, maybe he made a mistake, we got rid of him, okay, but we don't need to send him out in the rowboat on the lake with Al Neri, do we?"

Comey didn't understand. Which I found very strange, like maybe he was just playing dumb to embarrass me, because shouldn't an FBI director, of all people, know *The Godfather*s, at least the first two?

"What I mean, *James*," I said, "is I really hope you can see your way clear to letting this all go, letting Flynn go, investigation-wise, 'crime'-wise. He's a good guy. I really hope you can let this go, James. I really do."

Comey did his same old nervous headmaster blah-blah-blah protocol blah-blah-blah, with one of those I'm-sorry-but-I'm-so-pure smiles that have always pissed me off. Pardon my French.

War-gaming is part of my responsibility as commander in chief, which I take very seriously, extremely seriously, unbelievably seriously—and as Ivanka says, I've got unbelievable "visual intelligence."

THE SO-CALLED RUSSIA STORIES

I vanka and Jared each asked me yesterday, separately, if they could read what I've written so far.

"Not until I'm all done," I said. "Nobody but me reads it until the fall. I told your stepmother the same thing. And her 'advisers.'"

Actually, when I told the First Lady she couldn't read it, she thought I was saying she wouldn't be able to *understand* it, because of her English. Which made me chuckle, which made her say that not letting her read my book is like how I don't take my clothes off in front of her. It was just regular husband and wife stuff, and I forgave her before she returned to New York at the end of the weekend. (By the way, getting ready for bed in private is much, much more romantic in my opinion. The dark is romantic. I once asked Hugh Hefner about this, and he totally agrees—Hugh Hefner!)

"With the book," Jared said, "I just think you need to be especially careful concerning Russia."

"You don't need to worry about that," I told him. "I had a chat about it with McGahn [my White House lawyer]. I totally get that as president, regardless of any information I may transmit orally or in written form, I am not thereby waiving my executive privilege from disclosing to Congress or any court or tribunal information or records that may someday be requested or subpoenaed. I get that, Jared."

"Good," he replied.

"I'm almost not even mentioning Russia in the book. Except if I make peace with them."

"Great," Jared said. "That's terrific. I'm pleased. Ivanka will be, too. Everyone will be. Because for posterity, you know, as we've discussed, if you don't *mention* the untrue allegations, then when people read your book in ten years or twenty years, they'll think it was nothing. Because it *is* nothing."

"Right. I get that. Hardly any Russia in the book at all. Maybe one tiny chapter. Maybe not. I haven't decided. We'll see."

But *he* brought up the "posterity." This *is* history. This is *history*. I can't ignore it. If I left Russia and Putin out completely, the media and the historians would say, "Oh, look—Trump was hiding something, he was a puppet, he was scared." I'm not, I'm *so* not. In fact, it's the opposite: *Other people* are hiding so many things, *other people* are puppets, *other people* are scared.

So let me use this opportunity to lay out all the facts and come clean, once and for all. Not in a tweet. Not in an off-the-cuff answer at a press conference with the fake media, who are like assassins always trying to take shots at me. Here in a *book*.

Yes, the president of Russia, incredibly popular with his people and very tough with his enemies, said a few times that "Trump is a genius." Which gave the pathetic Democrats and the disgusting fake media an opening to start all the Russia talk after they blew the election, even though I don't know Putin at all. Until I was president, I hadn't even talked to Putin; I still haven't met him. I have no deals in Russia, zero investments, I've only been to the country for a couple of days for the great 2013 Miss Universe pageant that was held there. All the stories are based on zero proof, nothing but made-up facts by sleazy political operatives, all of them unverified and unverifiable. It's all a total ruse, a giant hoax, completely phony, 100 percent fake. Paul Manafort and Mike Flynn, who I guess had business dealings in that part of the world, worked for the campaign and, in Flynn's case

I AGREE THAT ALL THE PROMINENT RUSSIANS WHO'VE BEEN DYING THIS YEAR, LIKE ONE A WEEK, IS WEIRD.

for the Administration, very, very briefly, ridiculously briefly—because I *fired* both of them, and I'm almost certain I never even met that dopey Carter Page, the weak one who smiles all the time like the worst liar ever. I agree that all the prominent Russians who've been dying this year, like one a week, including the businessman I mentioned earlier, my personal lawyer's relative Alex (or Ivan or whatever)—Ukrainian, not Russian, but still—is weird. (My Secret Service guy Anthony says not to worry, but he'll ask about Geiger counters in the White House and Mar-a-Lago kitchens.) What is definitely horrible are the disgusting leaks by the "intelligence community," who are acting like the secret police in Russia when it was *really* bad, or Nazi Germany, and need to be prosecuted and locked up.

By the way, even if I'd wanted to have super top-secret private chats with Putin every couple of days on the famous "red phone," the hotline between the Oval Office and the Kremlin, which could be great, it turns out I can't. There is no red phone! Very disappointing. I wondered if maybe the "intelligence" guys were just keeping it from me because of the fake Russia stories, the way my dad used to lock up his secret stuff—which, just to keep me on the ball, he always claimed were my "adoption papers" and "IQ scores." But Ivanka and Jared confirmed it's true—no red phone at all, just an e-mail hookup, what the military calls the MOLINK. I thought they were making some kind of army joke, that Russians or presidents who use the system are gay, but it's short for Moscow Link. When I asked if it was used often, the colonel giving me the tour told me no, hadn't been used for years until last Halloween—when Obama sent Putin a message warning him that if they messed with the presidential election, America would consider it an act of war. Then I was *sure* he was joking, yanking my chain, hazing me. (But Ivanka looked it up on her Wikipedia—it's true! Isn't it amazing how scared the Democrats were of me winning? And setting up in advance their fake "Russia" excuse for losing?) My end of the MOLINK isn't even in the Oval Office—it's downstairs in the Situation Room, and runs from there over to the Pentagon and *then* to Russia. Which means it really is like how my dad used to lock things away and always kept the car keys in his pocket.

So that's what I have to say about Russia. The bottom line is, I don't really pay much attention to the so-called Russia stories about me and my campaign, because I've got so many, many more important things to deal with as president.

★ ★ ★ ★ ★ ★ ★ ★

IF I ACTED "PRESIDENTIAL" I'D LOSE MY SPECIAL POWERS

W hen I was president of The Trump Organization, growing it into an exceptional global business, among the world's best according to many experts, no executive of mine would dream of embarrassing me. And I don't mean just my children—I mean the people without any Trump genes whatsoever. So now as president of the *United States*, why do my guys second-guess me in public all the time? Especially the generals I hired for the non-general jobs—who I hired because I thought their whole attitude was loyalty, chain of command, obeying orders, yes, sir. So why does Homeland Security put out an untrue report about our ban on terrorist immigrants, claiming that "country of citizenship is unlikely to be a reliable indicator of potential terrorist activity"? When I announce we're deporting the baddest hombres back to Mexico in like a perfect military operation, why does my Homeland Security general have to say, "There will be no use of military in this"? One of the big Trump foreign policy principles, even before I was in politics, was that I would've taken all the oil from Iraq on our way out—so when my defense secretary goes to Abu Dhabi, why does he have to say, "We're not in Iraq to seize anybody's oil"? And *also* say on the same trip, we won't tear up the Iran deal, as I'd promised we would, because "we have to live up to it and work with our allies." As soon as I hired him, Mad Dog became Tame Dog, Nice Dog . . . Scooby-Doo? At least Mike Flynn never contradicted me—and then as soon as I give General McMaster Flynn's old job, why does he go all Hillary and announce that "radical Islamic terrorism" isn't a nice thing to say?

Wow, I just realized: At The Trump Organization, I wasn't only the *president*—I was also *chairman*. I'm going to have my White House lawyer look into whether or not we need a constitutional amendment so I can be president *and chairman* of the United States. I'm pretty sure we can just go ahead and do it by executive order, or maybe have Congress pass a bill to make it more official.

Speaking of making the government run more like a great business? In the executive order that's about to change the cabinet guys' titles, we're also going to tweak the White House branding. If the failing establishment doesn't want The Trump Organization to acquire the complex to make it as beautiful as it should be and lease it back to the government at cost for a limited period, fine—but we can still give the place some Trump flavor. Here's an exclusive sneak preview of the new logo that'll be going on every White House letterhead and Web site and sign and piece of merchandise very soon:

THE WHI**T**E HOUSE

WASHINGTON

Exclusive preview of our new White House logo.

Rodrigo told me he loves the new logo, by the way, especially the gold version. He also told me "Filipino" isn't racist, it's what you're supposed to say—even though it also always sounded to me like an SUV model, a cheap one, "the new…Chevy Filipino!" By the way, Trump is very, very popular among the Filipino Americans, amazingly popular, way beyond the other Oriental and minority communities—who, by the way, also voted for me much more than they did for Romney, which the fake media has covered up. As a White House employee, Rodrigo says he doesn't vote on principle, but his father and brother-in-law voted for me, although it was in California, so it didn't count. Sad.

★ ★ ★ ★ ★ ★ ★ ★ ★ ★ ★ ★ ★ ★ ★ ★ ★ ★ ★ ★

AS A BUSINESSMAN I was never like other businessmen, including being much, much more successful than 99 percent of them, but did anyone ever complain I wasn't "businesslike"? No, apart from a few incompetents and cheats whose ridiculous bills I negotiated. I wasn't like other people on prime-time TV, because every word they say is scripted for them and their shows never last for fifteen years, but nobody ever said I wasn't a huge *star*. Now I'm president—but because I'm different from any president ever, at least since log cabin times, the pundits and phonies and haters and elitists and fake media complain I'm not *presidential*." Which is offensive. To be perfectly honest, that's almost like a racist thing to say.

I prove them wrong over and over, of course. I can be presidential. It's the easiest thing in the world to be presidential. When I gave my first big speech to Congress, with the bouncing electronic ball added to my teleprompter screens (my invention, already applied for a patent), literally everybody was like, "Oh, look, he said 'our children will grow up in a nation of miracles'! Trump is *so* presidential, very presidential, completely presidential, he's amazing!"

Fine. But *nobody else* can be *Trump*! If I acted "presidential" all the time, I'd start losing my special powers, kind of like Superman if there were kryptonite powder mixed into all the paint everywhere in the White House—not enough to kill him but just enough to weaken him and turn him into a normal human. If I acted "presidential" all the time, the press and the haters would *pretend* not to hate me as much, but the people who really *love* Trump would start loving him less. Trust me on this.

"One of the most effective press conferences I've ever seen"— that's what the brilliant and legendary Rush Limbaugh, the No. 1 nonfake media anchorman in America, said about my first solo press conference as president. Thank you, Rush! But as always, the ups, as great as they are, only last a little while. Of course the rest of the media, the fake media, the lying media, the nasty un-American media said my press conference wasn't "presidential."

They say the way I tweet "isn't presidential." What they mean is that presidents aren't supposed to tell the straight truth the way I do—about crooked and disgusting Hillary, about dopey Obama, about the illegal "popular vote," about the illegal leaks and disgusting fake news and witch hunts. As I say, acting "presidential" is so easy—like on Twitter, when I want, I can go for several days at a time using no capital letters and being completely positive and nice, so positive and nice. If I want.

But I'm not dumb. I see what the Democrats and the media are up to when they start saying, "Oh, look, he's being *presidential*." It's like they're trying to get me drunk, seduce me, make me their puppet. They want me to take my eye off the ball—*balls*, plural, so many balls to juggle as president, important balls. Like after my great speech to Congress, they wanted me to ignore that they forced Jeff Sessions to "recuse" himself from the Russia hoax. But I didn't fall for their trick. Instead, I just picked up my phone and tweeted the truth. It means they don't think I'm being "presidential" again, because I'm showing my true self. I'm Trump. I only know how to do things one way, my way, the Trump way.

> *VOICE MEMO: Presidential to-do list*
> *Song, "DIDN'T FALL FOR THEIR TRICK / JUST*
> *PICKED UP MY PHONE AND TWEETED THE*
> *TRUTH / ONE WAY, MY WAY, THE TRUMP WAY,"*
> © 2017 *by Donald J. Trump.*

I'm not going to lie. For a day after my big speech to Congress, I was on top of the world. People said it was the best speech ever made in that chamber, a hole in one, a grand-slam home run, like being intimate with Ursula Andress from *Dr. No* and Princess Di at the same time. I'd convinced some of the sick haters that I deserved respect.

JEFF *IS* A LITTLE ON THE WEAK SIDE, I'M AFRAID, AND FOR ALL I KNOW HE'S GUILTY OF SOMETHING. TRUMP IS NOT GUILTY OF ANYTHING, OR WEAK.

But those were the same people who pushed Jeff Sessions to recuse, recuse, recuse, which would make Comey, and the FBI literally out of control—so the day after the speech to Congress I called Comey, I'm very nice, very respectful. "Mr. President," he said, "I can't tell you you're being investigated." I took that as a no, I wasn't being investigated, but then made him confirm it because he's a sneaky lawyer. When I told him again how important loyalty is in any organization, including the government, especially the government, he refused to get on board. And then the next day Jeff did recuse. Which was so wrong, because it made Jeff look weak and guilty. Which makes the president look weak and guilty. Jeff *is* a little on the weak side, I'm afraid, and for all I know he's guilty of something. Trump is not guilty of anything, or weak.

> *VOICE MEMO: Presidential to-do list*
> *Song, "HOLE IN ONE, GRAND-SLAM HOME RUN /*
> *PRINCESS DI, HONEY RIDER, BOTH AT ONCE,"*
> *© 2017 by Donald J. Trump. Kanye "rap" song???*

The afternoon Jeff recused while I was grabbing a snack (chicken tenders) in the restaurant in the West Wing basement—"eating your stress again," Ivanka always says—I ran into Mike Pence. Hadn't talked to him for quite a while, so I unloaded, told him I felt like hurting somebody. He smiled and nodded like the dads on TV shows when I was a kid, who always seemed so fake, or like the one "nice" coach we had at military school. "Well, Mr. President," he finally said, "the wiles of the devil can be seductive." I didn't know where he was going with that, so I stood and said "Amen, Mr. Vice President," which always makes Mike happy.

Back upstairs in the Oval, Reince tried to cheer me up, too. He knew my feelings about the White House servants—that except for Rodrigo, I felt I couldn't completely trust them because they don't work for *me* and can't really be fired on my say-so.

"Piece of good news, Mr. President. I found out you *can* terminate the chief usher anytime you want. She's not civil service."

"The Jamaican, the lady butler?" I asked. "Yeah, *right*. Maybe I 'can,' legally, but I'm sure Obama put her in there just to mess with me. She reminds me of Whitney Houston's mother. Did you know Whitney was my friend? Went to her wedding. I'd heard about the drugs, but I never knew she was broke. No wonder, though, with that terrible, terrible reality show she and the husband did, on cable, for peanuts, looked like crap. So sad. I was invited to the funeral. I couldn't make it. You know at the inauguration ball I had the band play 'I Will Always Love You' because she and I were close, right?"

"Yes, Mr. President."

"But the butler, you know, the Jamaican, she managed Ritz-Carltons, she might be one of the . . . what did you say it was? A quarter? How many of the blacks voted for Trump?"

"Eight percent, Mr. President."

"I think she could be one of those. Maybe you can look it up, confidentially. It'd be good to know if she was."

★ ★

NOW THAT I'VE BEEN LIVING in the White House for more than two months, including one of the last four weekends, I finally figured out one of my problems with it, aside from the major one of not owning it. In Trump Tower, it's like ninety seconds from the penthouse to The Trump Organization headquarters, straight shot, fast elevator, fantastic, almost like I just *think* myself from my bedroom to my office. In the White House, it's like some crazy obstacle course getting from where I live to where I work. The private elevator is small and slow and old-fashioned, European in the not-very-nice way. You may not realize that the West Wing, where the Oval Office is, is a whole separate building like half a block away, and walking outside on that colonnade, which can get extremely windy, right after spending a *lot* of time with the hair spray and combs and so forth, is just asking for trouble.

So last weekend when I stayed in Washington, my great African American Secret Service agent Anthony and I came up with a visionary solution to the problem. We plotted a new presidential route to work, a totally private route, the special Trump route. You know *Get Smart*, the original TV series from when we were kids? It's like the opening sequence of that, except very serious instead of funny, so more like a modern Batman movie if Bruce Wayne were elected president — which by the way is a great idea and hereby my copyrighted concept. So now every morning I'm in Washington, after I've had my seven pieces of crispy bacon, my American, non-Muslim version of Obama's seven almonds a day, and I've finished watching *Fox & Friends* and the failing bad shows on other channels during the ads on Fox, I take the elevator all the way down to the basement, then immediately step into what looks like a storage closet — but it's actually the secret entrance to a long underground tunnel to the West Wing. (They built it right before Bill Clinton got elected. I've heard he brought Monica down there, and I'm trying to get Anthony, my special agent, to confirm with his older buddies that Hillary used it for her own monkey business with her Middle Eastern assistant who married the pervert Anthony Weiner, which I've also heard.) At the very end of the tunnel is a staircase that leads up to a secret sliding door that opens — abracadabra, there I am, right between my Oval Office restroom and the Oval itself, my hair totally perfect, ready to command. Getting there that way feels very, very presidential. We're looking into having music piped into the tunnel, such as the *Mission: Impossible* theme, and also installing a moving walkway, like the ones at airports — which would be great, because then during the trip each morning I could get more tweeting done. Same thing when I knock off for the evening — as I'm doing right now, walking out of the Oval — good night, Hopester! — as I give dictation to Mitzi, writing this, my president book, making every second count.

I probably forgot to mention that I named my phone computer. I did that after I visited Ivanka and Jared's new house the other night. (Rental, five fireplaces, plain decor like they prefer, *very* nice deal, owner's from Chile but he's a billionaire, like me, and has big mining interests here, so he loves America.) I noticed Jared was shouting orders to somebody, but the babysitters and cook were nowhere in sight. "Who's Alexa?" Turns out it's their Amazon computer — like Siri in all the Apple phones, and Cortana in Sean Spicer's phone. The desk in the Oval Office has its own special name, Resolute, so I decided the president's phone

IT'S THE NAME OF THE FIRST GIRL I EVER KISSED, WHO SAID I HAD BAD BREATH AND THEN AFTER NINTH GRADE EITHER MOVED TO MANHATTAN OR DIED, I FORGET WHICH.

needed its own one-of-a-kind name, too. I picked Mitzi. It's an *M*-word, like all of the Trumps' Secret Service code names, and it's the name of the first girl I ever kissed, who said I had bad breath and then after ninth grade either moved to Manhattan or died, I forget which, but—*whoa*, Steve! You startled me.

I just came through the secret "closet" in the basement, and here's Steve Bannon waiting for me. He and my other Irishmen— General Kelly and Don McGahn—are about to take off with me for a guys' weekend at Mar-a-Lago. Plus Wilbur Ross, who's also Catholic and bought and sold half of Ireland the last few years. Hey, and now here's my fantastic *Kosher* Steve, who's flying with us—Kosher Steve is what I call Stephen Miller, who used to work for Sessions and also for Bannon at *Breitbart*. He's like Jared but scary—you are, man!—in a great way, a Roy Cohn way, he's even got Roy's eyes.

I just found out something very, very bad. I can't reveal exactly how I found out. But I'm president, and therefore I'm told a lot of secret things, very important secrets, many of them terrible secrets. I'm told that six weeks ago, the failing *New York Times* accidentally revealed this secret, and an extensive summary has just been posted on *Breitbart*. Wow.

Shooting another amazing
round at my fabulous
Trump International Golf
Club in West Palm
(which has the highest
elevation of any golf course
in Florida, by the way)
while an aide briefs me on
the global warming hoax.

THE AMERICAN PEOPLE UNDERSTAND

he birds are starting to make their noises. So many birds in Palm Beach.

The sun isn't up yet.

What I learned yesterday disturbed me so much I had a rough time sleeping, rougher than usual, only three hours instead of my usual four or five.

The kids and the First Lady aren't going to be happy. But none of them are here. And it's Saturday, so Vanks and Jared are on shutdown for Shmegegge until nighttime.

And if *I* don't tell the world, who will? As someone said yesterday on Air Force One, it's one of my destinies to be America's first whistle-blower in chief.

"Obama wiretapped me in Trump Tower last fall! My office! Possibly my private bedroom! But they found nothing, because NOTHING TO FIND, so couldn't prevent my landslide victory! As someone on AF One said, it's McCarthyism!"

Need to trim eighty-one characters. *Tweet.*

I see sunlight.

"When a SECRET COURT turns down your 'wiretap,' even if you're the sitting 'President,' OBAMA, I'm pretty sure it's ILLE-GAL to go ahead and 'wiretap' a campaign for president before an election! DISGUSTING NEW LOW!"

I probably shouldn't include his name. Ivanka and Jared and the First Lady will hate that. Also, it's seventy-five long. Okay, trim. *Tweet.*

The sun is up. I feel a little better. And I know I'll feel even better if I do name him.

"It's disgusting and historic what President Obama did—to tapp my private personal telephones during our highly sacred election procedure. Much, much, much worse than Nixon & Watergate. Very bad (or VERY SICK) dude!"

Tweak, trim, and . . . *tweet*, wham bam!

> *MITZI: Presidential to-do list*
> *Song, "TWEAK, TRIM, AND TWEET / WHAM BAM,"*
> © *2017 by Donald J. Trump, add to Kanye rap song.*

When you have as many followers on Twitter as I do, as soon as each tweet gets beamed up, it's amazing to watch the "likes" and "retweets" roll in, live tallies, like a hundred a minute. Sometimes, quite frankly, I lose track of time watching that, realize a half hour has gone by and the meeting with the intelligence briefer or whatever is suddenly over. It's what Tiger Woods means when he talks about "getting in the zone."

I feel much, much better now.

In the bathroom I see another important piece of news that demands a response—Arnold Schwarzenegger is now pretending he *quit* as host of *New Celebrity Apprentice* because of the show's "baggage." The president of the United States is "baggage"?! So rude and unpatriotic, especially for an immigrant allowed to become an American without any vetting, even though his father was a Nazi. I need to tell the world that Arnold was fired because of his ratings.

I know the haters and pundits are going to hit me now for hitting Arnold right after I revealed that Obama committed major federal crimes and may be mentally ill—the ratings of a TV show, they'll say, aren't as "important" as my exposé of this terrible secret attack on our election process. To that I have three answers. First, both are about *telling the truth*, which Donald Trump happens to believe the American people deserve to know. Second, any president has to be a world-class "multitasker," as Ivanka says, dealing with a completely different kind of problem every minute—and then be able to leave it all behind and clear his head as he tees off—at 9 a.m. sharp—on the fabulous first hole of Trump International Golf Club in West Palm Beach. And third— morning, Anthony, how's it hangin'? . . . third, whatever it was I'll remember and talk about later.

★ ★ ★ ★ ★ ★ ★ ★ ★ ★ ★ ★ ★ ★ ★ ★ ★ ★ ★ ★

I SHOT A FIFTY-NINE this morning, one of my best scores ever. It's freaky how well I've been playing. *Two* holes in one today, one of them on a par four, birdies and eagles on most of the others, which is so incredible, almost, what do you call it, *supernatural*. It made me think that all that praying for me, from all those millions and millions and millions of Christians all over America, is actually *working*. I'd ask Mike Pence, but then he'd start in. Anyhow, it's a shame that issuing press releases or even mentioning my scores on Twitter would be "bragging." I think it would cheer up America—we're *winning!*—but Ivanka and everybody says no.

I was in a fantastic mood when my African American Secret Service agent Anthony and I walked into the Mar-a-Lago Club tonight. "What the heck, *Willll*-bur," I said to my commerce secretary/SVP biz dev, Wilbur Ross. Everyone at the presidential table chuckled. "This was supposed to be a guys' weekend—who's this hot tamale you brought along for us? She's just the right height for Jeff!" Everyone laughed hard, including Mrs. Ross, whose name is actually Hillary. "Pardon my French"—I whispered, but *loud*, you know—"who doesn't like to *fuck* a *Hillary*, huh?" Pardon my French, but they laughed hard! I've known Wilbur and Hillary for years. She's his third. Most of us are on our thirds— me and Mnuchin (treasury secretary/EVP finance), Bannon has had at least three. For almost seventy, Hillary Ross looks fantastic, an eight or probably a nine for her age, which by the way is another way I'm actually *so nice* to women—over forty, I have a very fair formula in my head for calculating their scores, like handicaps in golf.

You know how Abe Lincoln had his "team of rivals"? I didn't either until I heard Charles Krauthammer or some professor mention it on Fox while I was picking my cabinet. That's why I did the favor for Ben Carson, one reason, but not many people know that Wilbur Ross was also once one of my tough, tough rivals. It's too complicated to explain all the details, but *way* back, during the first Bush Administration, some Wall Street types expected me to pay a ridiculously unfair interest rate on $675 million they'd invested in my fantastic Trump Taj Mahal casino. Wilbur was their guy, and the two of us negotiated a very, very nice deal where Donald Trump, the person, didn't declare bankruptcy, because I never have and never will, and everybody got to walk away happy.

I sat down at the table, but something didn't feel right, like something was out of balance, and then I realized the problem. I made everybody change seats so that it would be me, then a bald guy (General Kelly), then another guy with great hair (Don McGahn), almost-bald guy (Kosher Steve), another guy with great hair (Bannon), bald guy (Ross), woman with nice hair, Jeff Sessions. I think Bannon thought I did it because I didn't want him next to me.

"Hey," I said, "offense is the only good defense, right?" We were discussing how I'd called out Obama that morning for wiretapping me. The two Steves totally loved the tweets. Wilbur said the follow-up right afterward with Schwarzenegger proved I wasn't "obsessed with the Russia stuff." McGahn rained on the parade a little, but he's a lawyer, and both Steves swore up and down that the writer of the *Breitbart* article about the Obama wiretaps is a very strong guy, their most trusted guy, Harvard and Harvard Law School, and that for sure there was all kinds of proof, confidential sources, et cetera.

"Right, General Kelly?" I said to my Homeland Security SVP. "You worked for Obama—they probably wiretapped you, too, when you hit them on Guantanamo and letting ladies in the infantry, am I right?"

Kelly just smiled and shrugged.

"Well, Mr. President," my counsel said, "it was good you put quotation marks in the tweets around 'wiretapping.' That gives us some definitional leeway."

"Right," I said. "Exactly right, Don. Important point. In fact, that's one of the reasons I use quotation marks so much in the tweets, like with 'rigged' and 'dudes' and 'evil.' The extra spice and punch but also that definitional leeway, I love the definitional leeway."

Bannon chuckled, which made me wonder if he thinks I didn't know what "definitional leeway" meant. Steve is tough but he can also be kind of a prick sometimes.

"The other thing," I said, "is that I could have gone so much farther than I did. I could have gone public about the weird beeping Tiffany's iPad made that day in Cleveland during the convention when she tried watching the big video by Obama and Hillary's friend Beyoncé. I could have gone public about Barron's school having a teacher whose father was a bigwig in the CIA under Bush. I could have gone public about the window washer incident." The Rosses hadn't heard about the window washer. "At Trump Tower, day before the election, twenty-sixth floor, right there on the other side of the glass, an Arab guy, earphones

I COULD HAVE GONE PUBLIC ABOUT THE WEIRD BEEPING TIFFANY'S IPAD MADE THAT DAY IN CLEVELAND DURING THE CONVENTION WHEN SHE TRIED WATCHING THE BIG VIDEO BY OBAMA AND HILLARY'S FRIEND BEYONCÉ.

with red wires leading to something in his pocket. I had Anthony take care of him. We kept that one quiet."

Everybody was sort of looking at their plates. They were probably nervous that a waiter might overhear top-secret things.

"Hey," I said to my attorney general, "you're being awful quiet over there. Cat got your tongue, Mr. Mouse?" Sessions looks like a talking mouse in a cartoon, right? "Just because you '*recused*' on investigating the campaign doesn't mean you can't talk about it! Right, Don? No? Okay, Jeff, plug your ears! Better yet— Hillary, take the attorney general down to a cabana for a few minutes, teach him how to be a real man. Kidding!" I've stopped calling him "Jeffy" ever since he recused. Management 101. By the way, those eight cabanas on the beach for Mar-a-Lago Club members are unbelievably lavish.

Don was still worried the media and the Democrats in Congress would keep demanding "proof" that Obama did to me even worse than what Hillary and the Democrats claim the Russians did to her. "I've got it," I said. "The letter he left for me in the Oval. Obama admits the whole thing in there. And apologizes for it."

For like five seconds, maybe ten, nobody said a thing.

"I'm not saying he *did* say that in the letter," I continued, "not in so many words, like in a deposition or something. But I could say my strong belief is he basically confirmed it in the letter."

Don was shaking his head. "Obama would deny it immediately."

"So?" I said. "It was handwritten. You think he made a photocopy? I doubt it. And I say I can't show it because of executive privilege. No? Then because it's private and confidential. Like my taxes."

Don was shaking his head again. "Obama says, 'Go ahead, Mr. President, you have my permission—release the letter I wrote you.'"

Okay, Obama didn't say "Hey, Don, I wiretapped you, sorry about that." He's a writer, he's a lawyer, he's clever, he's sneaky. But someday, when all the papers are in the archives, historians will see that between the lines he was definitely confessing.

My good mood was over. Likc I say, the ups never last long. It's always something. "Well, Bannon," I told him, "this started with you. You called it—what did you say—'a huge attack on democracy,' 'the largest abuse of power ever.' So if we have a problem it's your problem. Up to you to back it up, gather up the evidence, find the proof."

★ ★

I STARTED THIS MORNING with another *up* at Trump International Golf Club. Four hours playing on one of my fantastic courses is as perfect as life gets, like I'm dreaming—actually like heaven as heaven has been advertised all these years. There are ten reasons for this, which I considered turning into its own book, *Donald Trump's Guide to Heaven on Earth* or *Heaven Is for Winners*, but I don't have the time, so I'm giving it to you here at no extra charge.

First of all, I own the course, which is wonderful for me. Second, it's beautiful in a way *everybody* thinks is beautiful, not like Angelina Jolie who to me looks like the young Martin Landau, or like one of those artworks that some people *say* are beautiful but most people know really aren't. Third, it's perfectly groomed, which you could say is part of beauty, but to me it's so important it's a separate thing. Fourth, you're with guys who either paid $250,000 to join and $30,000 a year to play or friends of those guys—people who want the best. Fifth, the caddies—a lot of them African American and Hispanic, doing a simple job well, very polite, quiet unless you ask them something, for only $100 a day—what I spend every *second*, which is amazing, right? Sixth, you hit a thing so hard with a steel club that if it were alive you'd kill it, but then on the green you just tap it and it does exactly what you want and disappears. Seventh, there are no surprises on a golf course you've played a hundred times, and almost nobody ever says anything you don't understand. On the other hand, my eighth point: It doesn't all come easy—and I don't mean just the sand traps and water hazards, which are real challenges but also beautiful and perfectly groomed in their own right. I mean challenging like our fifth hole at Trump International in West Palm Beach, where the fairway narrows and the vegetation gets very dense

THERE ARE NO SURPRISES ON A GOLF COURSE YOU'VE PLAYED A HUNDRED TIMES, AND ALMOST NOBODY EVER SAYS ANYTHING YOU DON'T UNDERSTAND.

and thick with the palm trees, almost *dark*, like in the African jungle, and you're an explorer, where natives could suddenly come out of the trees and attack you, and the caddies might help fight them off *or* might run away *or*, scariest of all, suddenly feel like chumps and join up with the natives and massacre you. Ninth, there's a happy ending: After you go past the beautiful two-story waterfall we built on the seventeenth hole, the clubhouse comes into view, which is home sweet home, with the marble foyer, the big gold and crystal chandelier, the antique statues of baby angels, and the greatest onion rings in Florida, probably in America. Lastly, number ten, somebody wins, and usually it's me.

In fact, this morning it was even more like heaven than usual, because I shot even better than yesterday—fifty-seven, with two holes in one and like ten inches short of a third. I think three is the all-time world record, which I asked Anthony, my great African American special agent, to Google on the way back to Mar-a-Lago. By the way, Anthony finally admitted he didn't vote for me, but he swore to me he didn't vote for Hillary either, it was the first time he didn't vote for president, which actually made me choke up.

Anthony looks so great, so fit, so hard, so tough, I've decided I want my entire Secret Service detail to be all African Americans all the time. Which would be such a win-win—highlighting my civil rights reputation and also extra scary to any bad guys thinking of attacking me. Anthony told me there are like three hundred black special agents. It's a visionary idea, so people will complain, but it's totally doable. Exciting, right?

But then I came home and watched all the Sunday shows I'd TiVo'd. They were bad, so bad, so full of weakness for our side. Of course all the fake media reporters and pundits came out against me on my tweets about Obama wiretapping. Of course Obama's "intelligence" chief Clapper—what a name, huh?—and of course Obama's Democrat CIA guy Panetta came on the shows to go against me.

The only person who works for Trump we put on any of the shows on any of the channels, including Fox, is Mike Huckabee's daughter? Nice girl, more calm than Sean, I don't have Ivanka's issue about her weight, but all she does this morning is keep repeating about the wiretrapping, "It was on the BBC, it was in the *New York Times*." Then the elderly guy who was W's attorney general for a year, pal of Giuliani's, he's supposed to be on *our* side and goes on TV saying, "I don't do tweets" and "tweets are bad" and "somebody in Trump Tower may have been a Russian agent" and "there's nothing to prosecute except the Russians"?

And the senators they had on, my *Republican* fucking senators from the intelligence committee, pardon my French? That you-know-what Susan Collins says "no evidence," "Trump should turn over any evidence, better yet Trump should just shut up," so disrespectful. (By the way, Reince just told me she got married for the first time four years ago, at like sixty. Wow. Never heard of a woman doing that.) The kid Cotton from Oklahoma, suppos- edly conservative—"I've seen no evidence," "I ignore Trump's tweets." And little fucking Marco Rubio, pardon my French—I give him a nice tweet when he's begging to get back in the Senate after I beat him, two days ago I give him a nice ride down here to Florida on Air Force One, find him salsa in the galley for his beautiful in-flight shrimp, and now on Sunday this is what he does to me? I've always said Marco was a very dishonest and disloyal lightweight little boy, but he was the worst about the Obama wire-tapping, he went on and on, on *Meet the Press* and also CNN— "no evidence, no one's presented anything; never seen anything anywhere about that; never heard that from anybody; ask Trump, he'll answer it, make him explain; I'm not the guy that went out and said that." Fuck me, I am going to fuck that motherfucking little Cuban choker so bad when he runs against me in 2020, pardon my French. The little Spanish fuck. Pardon my French.

The American people understand what's going on. They know. This is why I won, even though it's literally impossible for a Republican to win in the electoral college. The people know all the professional politicians in Washington are scared of the truth, scared of somebody in power who knows the score, scared of me. The people hate the "elite" and now they hate that the elite is trying to make Trump look stupid and dishonest, and make him feel bad. I refuse to let the corrupt elite establishment insiders force me to let the American people down.

★ ★ ★ ★ ★ ★ ★ ★ ★

A GOOD TEST FOR COMEY

I gave Rodrigo a new title, senior steward and special international minority adviser to the president—secret for now so the press won't jump all over us. (Before the promotion I did some security double-checking on Rodrigo through Anthony, my African American special agent, and he's an A-plus.) By the way, Rodrigo doesn't think the new executive order for extreme vetting we issued today is "racist." He's completely for it. There are *millions* of Muslims in the Philippines, which many people don't know, actually even more than in America, and they came in hundreds of years ago, before any kind of vetting had been set up. They all live down on the real jungle islands, which many people also don't know, a thousand miles from beautiful Trump Tower Manila, which is great, because no roads connect, but they're still a big, big, major problem for the country—uneducated, poverty, violence, worse than Chicago, riots, radical Islamic, carnage. I'm going to brief my "intelligence" briefers about this at my next "briefing." In the fall I'm going to the Philippines for a big summit with all the countries down there, and I'll be meeting with

President Duty-Free of the Philippines. Duty-Free is a very strong supporter of Trump, very tough guy, he's taking care of his drug dealers big-league, used to do it personally. The "Asian Trump" they're calling him, which really shows you how hot the brand is in politics now all over the world. Ivanka thinks it's okay in those situations that they're using the brand without paying a license fee, because they'll be paying in other ways, and I guess she's probably right.

But speaking of the Pacific people and the island people—as Rodrigo says, it's not right to "stereotype," some are light and some are dark, some are good, some are bad, some are strong, some are weak. But *Hawaii* sued America today to stop our new, better ban on terrorist immigrants. *Hawaii*, remember, was foreign until we let it join America when I was in seventh grade—like a year before Obama was "born" "there," by the way, interesting "coincidence." And the Hawaiian attorney general who just sued us is named General *Chin*, I swear, and the federal judge who blocked us there is an Oriental, too, last name Watson but giveaway middle name, *Kahala*. Maybe I should let Kim Jong-un take Hawaii out and *then* nuke North Korea. (That's sarcasm. But that's also the way it could actually go down. That's actually a "scenario" I heard about from Mad Dog or one of the generals in his uniform, I forget which.) But also, seriously? The other federal judge who blocked the new vetting rules, in Maryland, is Judge *Chuang*. I mean, come *on*. You do have to wonder if this is a long-term play by China—get their guys in place in America, then bust my balls just for fun. China is smart.

> *MITZI: Presidential to-do list*
> *Emperor Xi next month, after a drink, let him know*
> *I know about the judges, watch his reaction.*

Jeff Sessions was just in here telling me he was nervous about having FBI counterintelligence in Hawaii check out my China theory. "It'd be a good test for Comey," I said, and after I gave him my "stay strong, tough guy" talk and the special handshake, he promised to do what he could about our Hawaii problems. I'm not quoting him, because I turned off the phone recorder because of something Jeff said about "the big mistake Mr. Nixon made." I also told him to look into whether that Hawaiian judge or their attorney general had some conflict from back when we were building the Trump International down there. Then I turned my recorder back on—I now do it just by reaching into my suit pocket and pressing the button, as I'm talking, very discreet.

"Or maybe those guys have been involved in some Honolulu monkey business before," I told him. "Maybe they fucked me in the Trump Waikiki deal." Pardon my French. "Maybe we can find out. Understand?"

He saluted me, which is a thing he does. It's cute.

"Whoa," I said, "this really has turned into a regular hula-hula pupu platter day at the White House, huh?"

"Mr. President?"

"Pupu platter, Hawaiian, you eat it? You don't have that in Alabama?"

He was confused but he seemed interested. We went back and forth like this for another minute, and I don't want to embarrass the attorney general with every detail, although someday I might. Bottom line is he thought "pupu platter" was a sex thing. This is another example of how people would like Jeff Sessions more if they got to know him. He's got his wild side, like a lot of the smaller guys do.

★ ★ ★ ★ ★ ★ ★ ★ ★ ★ ★ ★ ★ ★ ★ ★ ★ ★ ★ ★

I'M REALLY GLAD I've got Rodrigo with me, because something's going on with the Asians. And I don't just mean the ones in Hawaii.

Late last night I'm in the White House, alone upstairs in the Treaty Room, news shows all reruns so I'm watching Fallon's monologue, in the bathrobe, the bowl of Lays, the glass of Diet Coke—and suddenly my Special Service secret agent Anthony rushes into the room with his pistol drawn.

"*Mogul is secure*," he said into his cuff. That's my code name. Then he told me, "Intruder on the grounds, Mr. President," and just a few seconds later, he said, "Intruder apprehended at the South Portico, sir."

See, *that* is what makes being the president of the United States fun. *That* was what it's supposed to be, like in the movies. But actually so rare.

Also, by the way, when I say I'm the least racist person ever, that incident last night really proved it: A young black guy runs into my den without warning, holding a pistol, and I was completely fine with it.

Anthony and all the special agents carry a Sig Sauer P229. Great pistol. Big pistol. Before I was president, I carried a Glock 43— small and lightweight, fantastic little pistol. I've had a New York City concealed-carry permit almost forever, which is very hard to get, almost impossible, but I have one.

But back to the Vietnamese guy, the intruder—he's a computer engineer from Silicon Valley. Anthony's supervisor tells me the guy was actually carrying an Apple computer with him.

"Very interesting," I said. "Very, very interesting." What I meant was that this kid could be one of Obama's wiretappers. Just two days before, I'd switched to an Apple iPhone. Wow. *Wow*.

Then they tell me on his computer he had a letter addressed to me about "Russian hackers," and also a copy of one of my best-selling books. And *then* I find out he worked for one of the very major manufacturers of computer chips and security devices, the biggest *German* one, a company that Russian intelligence hates. And it manufactures computer chips—in *Tijuana*, in *Mexico*. Wow! This morning my son Barron said the guy was probably a *ninja*, and told me that one of the girls who assassinated Kim Jong-un's brother the other day was Vietnamese. Now it was even more like a movie, but one of the ones where I lose track, like *The Usual Suspects*, or the Bourne movie where Edward R. Murrow is tracking Matt Damon. I can't tell you more, or what the Vietnamese ninja's letter said, but I think we all probably have a pretty good idea what's going on. The ninja is back home in Silicon Valley, with a government monitor attached to him. And we're making the White House fence twice as high. I'll leave it at that for now.

130

I asked my Secret Service agent Anthony to show me his Sig Sauer P229 pistol—then ran a surprise drill, testing how he'd neutralize an attacking terrorist or Democrat.

131

★ ★ ★ ★ ★ ★ ★ ★

THEY SAID IT ON THE NEWS

I'll get to my big White House meeting with the German prime minister or president or whatever she is, but I'm not going to let the fake media bury this story of the illegal and disgusting surveillance of me by U.S. "intelligence" last fall and for all we know right now. Every time I ask, Anthony and the other special secret agents and their boss all tell me that the Southern White House and the White House and the Northern White House (Trump Tower) are clean. But I've ordered them to start "sweeping" more often.

Because I'm right about the wiretaps.

I know it. I *feel* it, in an unbelievably strong way, incredibly strong, fantastically strong. Earlier I mentioned my "superpower"—how I can tell who's a winner and who's not, or know when real estate values are about to go up or down, or if a woman has feelings for me even before she knows it herself. I realize now I've also always had another kind of superpower that lets me know when I'm being spied on. Ivanka says maybe I'm "alert to different energies," and Mike Pence calls them my "gifts of the Holy Spirit." The First Lady once said I'm like a dog who feels earthquakes beforehand, which frankly I found disgusting—the dog part—so she changed it to a unicorn—and about the wiretaps, she just mentioned that in Slovenia there's something called "incubus" that can change shape to anything, like even a hair or a crumb, and then insert itself anywhere. Scary.

I called my team into the Oval—Irish Steve and Kosher Steve, Irish Don, some of the other young guys, Reince, Jared. "I'm right about the surveillance, aren't I? I know I am. I mean, I know it wasn't necessarily a 'wiretap,' which is why I put the 'quotes' around it, definitional leeway, but otherwise, if anybody thinks the *Breitbart* geniuses led me in the wrong direction, speak up. Seriously."

I thought Jared was going to say something, but he didn't. Nobody didn't think I had it right.

"Well, Sean is doing the best he can every day, but we need more people like him out there doing their jobs, saying I'm right. Why aren't our intelligence committee guys, Burr in the Senate and what's his name in the House, the Californian, the Mexican, Núñez—why aren't they backing me up on this? They're basically saying I'm wrong. You guys need to fix this."

"It's *New-ness*, Mr. President, Devin Nunes, Portuguese ancestry?" Reince said, like a question, to let me know he'd told me that before, which I found very annoying. "No squiggle over the *n*?"

I didn't say anything for like five seconds; just shot him a look until his lips twitched. Leadership 101.

MITZI: Presidential to-do list
Song, "NO SQUIGGLE OVER THE N MAKES
AMERICA GREAT / SOMETHING SOMETHING,
ET CETERA," © 2017 by Donald J. Trump.

"Well," I said, "we need to turn Congressman *New-ness* into a team player. He's just a congressman, right, squeezably soft in the cojones department?"

Both of the Steves and my White House lawyer Don turned to look at this young guy I don't really know who was standing at the edge of the group. Bannon called him "Little Mikey," and said, "Mikey'll eat it." (From that Life cereal commercial—which I loved because we had a kid like that on our block in Queens, got him to jump off his roof holding two helium balloons, cracked open his head, *hilarious*.) I had my doubts, but then somebody said our Mike was a big winner on *Jeopardy!*, which I found very impressive. Also, he was Núñez's lawyer on the intelligence committee for a couple of years until we hired him.

I smiled and did my "thumbs-up" thing to that kid and Bannon and a couple of the others, a thumb for each one—which really excites people when I do it up close, face-to-face, because they've seen it so much on TV and in pictures. Management 101. It's like a logo, but *whoa*, there it is in real life, and it's amazing, like when a child sees a Santa for the first time, a good one, or if Mr. Peanut unexpectedly walked into a room, which happened to me once. It's the same thing as at rallies when I say one of my catchphrases, like "the failing *New York Times*," the crowds go crazy, like they do at Ted Nugent's concerts when he plays "Cat Scratch Fever." Leadership 101. You'd think I could definitely trademark the Trump Thumbs-Up, legally, right, as my branded thing? A few years ago the bureaucrats told us no, but Wilbur Ross is in charge of the Trademark Office now and he's circling back on that for me.

"By the way," I asked the room, "do any of you technology geniuses know about 'the incubus'? In Eastern Europe? Changes shape and slips in anywhere, almost invisible?"

★ ★ ★ ★ ★ ★ ★ ★ ★ ★ ★ ★ ★ ★ ★ ★ ★ ★ ★ ★

"RODRIGO?" It was the next morning. I was in the Treaty Room as usual, eating my bacon, drinking my Ovaltine, looking at my Twitter, reading the *New York Post*, watching *Fox & Friends*, normal morning. And then suddenly—*wow*. I still can't quite believe he actually did it. "*Rodrigo*—get in here and do playback of the last couple minutes of *Fox & Friends*, okay?"

Judge Napolitano, one of the very top, top, top legal analysts in the United States, revealed that Obama had gotten *British* intelligence to wiretap me, so there wouldn't be any "American fingerprints" on it, and then "provided Obama with transcripts of Trump's calls." It wasn't just his "opinion," he said they had three sources in the CIA or wherever, sources that "informed Fox News" that I was right. *They said it on the news.*

Home run, touchdown, hole in one! Trump wins again! When Rupert promised me after Roger Ailes had to leave that Fox News would be even more fair and more balanced when covering Trump, he wasn't kidding! I knew Judge Nap to be a wise man, a truthful man, extremely truthful, but now he's really a national hero. By the way, some people think he's some kind of *People's Court* guy, but he was a very respected actual judge in New Jersey back when I was in the casino business there, before he moved into my Trump International Hotel and Tower on Central Park West, the place where Mitt Romney failed his interview for secretary of state. Now that I really see how brave and committed to the truth Judge Nap is, I'm going to let him go ahead and put together that federal 9/11 commission redo he wants. He's been saying for years the attacks couldn't have happened the way the government said, and I'm sure he's right, but now we'll finally have an honest investigation to get the truth out.

Now we were on a roll uncovering the horrible wiretapping Obama did to me, like the gestapo in Nazi Germany or when Khrushchev ran Russia, terrible, the worst. The next day I went out for three hours to take care of all our great autoworkers in Michigan and then did a fantastic interview with Tucker Carlson for Fox News.

Tucker asked me about my amazing tweets about the wiretapping, and I reminded him about the "quotes" around wiretap, and Fox ran my complete answer, because they're fair. And then I finished with what we call in television a "tease," which I learned from those fifteen record-breaking seasons of *The Apprentice* and *Celebrity Apprentice*. You let the audience know something very exciting is coming in the next show without saying exactly what it is. I totally improvised, because that's what Trump does, but it was like a perfect putt, right into the hole from 100 yards — which by the way I've actually done, literally, golfing. "I think," I told Tucker about the disgusting surveillance of me, "you're going to find some very interesting new items coming to the forefront in the next two weeks." I try to do this every day, announcing to the world, "*Stand by, folks*," and they're like excited monkeys at the zoo, waiting for the next banana. Very powerful Leadership 101 stuff.

The next day, right after Sean went out and read Judge Nap's whole transcript to all the reporters, word for word, about the British spying on me and no fingerprints, I had him come into the Oval Office alone. He was so nervous.

"Sean?" I said.

"Yes, Mr. President?"

"I love that you go out there and do whatever it takes, whatever I say, you're a good soldier, the best. You just keep marching and chanting, like we did in military school, 'Whip me, beat me, I need love, let me feel that leather glove, whip it around, make it crack, lay that whip across my back.' No matter how much shit the reporters are throwing at you—keep going right up the beach, like that scene in *Saving Private Ryan*."

"I appreciate that, Mr. President."

"No matter what I said in January about the way you dressed, Sean, you're a hero." I handed him one of the metal four-leaf clover pins for the St. Patrick's Day event later on. "This is like your special Purple Heart, okay? Except green."

He teared up. Management 101.

It's Marketing 101 that when you're on a roll, you have to keep your eye on the ball and keep it rolling—even when other things are distracting you. Like when President Merkel came by the next day.

Meeting her in person, I realized that one of my big problems with her is that she reminds me of Hillary. She could be her sister, the hair so similar, dresses like her, really *behaves* like Hillary, thinks she's so smart and always acts like what I'm saying is ridiculous, comes across as so mean, like she's ready to scold me. As Steve Bannon says about Hillary, "You send a letter addressed to 'Bitch, Westchester, USA,' it gets delivered to her." Of course, she lost, big-time, electoral college landslide, a win for me that was literally impossible for a Republican, although I did it, which is so amazing.

But I was nice to Merkel. Beforehand I practiced pronouncing her name right. You don't say it like the beautiful redhead supermodel Angie Everhart, who I knew when I was single, or like Angela Lansbury—who, by the way, could be Hillary and Merkel's mother. It's AHHHHNGLE-uh, like the doctor's sticking the Popsicle stick down your throat, AHHHHNGLE-uh.

"So, *Angela*," I said, breaking the ice, so much ice with her, "Obama wiretapped you, Obama wiretapped me, we've got a lot in common, right?" She smiled in that polite, mean way. "But seriously, *Angela*, that kind of wiretapping—it makes you feel like we're living in Nazi Germany, right? Which I know you didn't, but you know, I'm German, my grandparents, my dad was actually, what do you call it, a fetus in Germany, but they tell me you're *East* Germany. Which is actually something I happen to like. The First Lady is from Slovenia,

MY DAUGHTER TIFFANY ENDS IN Y, WHICH IS ALSO CONSIDERED A VOWEL, NOT MANY PEOPLE KNOW THAT.

also Eastern Europe, right, Russia used to run it, and my first wife, Ivana, Czechoslovakia during the Communist time, right next to East Germany, as you know. So you and I should have a special feeling. And also, even your name, *Angela*—you probably didn't realize *all* my wives' names end in the letter *A*, and my daughter's also. And my daughter Tiffany ends in *Y*, which is also considered a vowel, not many people know that, plus all three of my granddaughters' names end in vowels. It's become kind of a family requirement, like the Kardashians with the *K*s. So all the beautiful girls in my life—and now you!"

Sometimes some of the supplements and special vitamins I take make me a little more talkative, which people actually love, since I don't drink.

When I asked Merkel if she ever met Putin when he was stationed in East Germany with the KGB, she said no and then changed the subject to economics and trade. She claimed we couldn't do a deal, America with Germany, because Germany's part of the European Union. *What?* Like NAFTA means I can't do a trade deal without getting permission from the Mexicans? *Please.*

But if she wanted to play hardball, Trump can play hardball. "Do you know your company, the German company, Infineon Technologies?"

"Yes, perhaps," she said, "I think maybe." I could tell she was pretending not to know. Standard negotiating trick. One of her guys piped up and reminded her she'd visited its factory in Dresden.

"Right," I said. "Okay, well, the Vietnamese guy who broke into the White House last weekend, you heard about that? Carrying a computer? And some messages about hacking and Russia? He works for Infineon Technologies."

And then she just completely played dumb, like she was confused, "No idea what you're talking about, Mr. President," and said she hadn't even seen the news about the ninja wiretapper arrested at the White House. Whatever. That's negotiation. You don't say everything you know.

But then after we sat for pictures by the fireplace in the Oval, the fake media made a big deal about me not shaking her hand. Why didn't I? I'll tell you why. Not because I was in a bad mood or don't like her. I shake hands with people I don't like all the time. It was because about thirty seconds before that, she went to the ladies' room, okay? Between that and the Hillary look-alike issue, I just couldn't bring myself to do it right then. Sorry for being human. It's like Shakespeare said in one of his most famous plays.

Hold on.

> *MITZI: Presidential to-do list*
> *Book fact-check, Shakespeare Jewish line Jared quoted*
> *at dinner on Purr him the other night, "I MAY BE A*
> *PRICK, BUT DON'T I STILL BLEED?" or whatever.*

As Merkel was leaving, by the way, I let her know I'm germo-phobic—but she thought I said *German*-phobic, so then we had to straighten that out, and *then* she said, "Freudian slip!" Which I guess meant she thought I was making some kind of sex joke, which I definitely wasn't, so I just smiled and said bye.

But later I did get in a bad mood. I found out that during my press conference with her, *right when* I was answering some German reporter about Obama using the British NSA to spy on me, and giving credit to Fox News, this guy Shemp Smith on Fox News *retracted* it, completely threw Judge Nap under the bus. "Fox News cannot confirm Judge Nap's commentary." And then Shemp Smith hits *me*, goes "Fox News knows of no evidence of any kind that the now president of the United States was sur-veilled at any time, in any way, full stop." This is a guy named after one of the Three Stooges, and not even one of the original, actual Three Stooges.

> *MITZI: Presidential to-do list*
> *Book fact-check, Fox News gay guy, "Shemp" or*
> *"Shep"? like the older cook at Mar-a-Lago says*
> *"shimfs" when he's talking about shrimp, "we got us*
> *some fine shimfs in today, Mister President"? Fantastic*
> *guy, African American, definitely voted for Trump,*
> *helped me win Florida.*

Okay, it's Shep. I'm sure he timed his attack on me and Judge Nap for when I was with Merkel, so that I couldn't see it live and react right away. When I called Rupert from Air Force One on the way to Palm Beach, he more or less apologized, and said even though he had to let his son pull Judge Nap off the air, it would only be for like a week. I reminded Rupert that I'd done what he wanted about so many things. Rupert just turned eighty-six, which worries me, quite frankly, because I'm not comfortable with the idea of the sons being totally in charge of Fox News, and I'm not sure Fox viewers would be either. For instance, I know about 90 percent of them agree with me about Obama's disgusting surveillance of me.

I spent nine hours that weekend at my Trump International Golf Club in West Palm Beach, where I had some important presidential meetings I'm not allowed to talk about, and also golfed, which lifted my mood, which is so important for the country — I shot below par on every hole, what they call a "perfect round," although this was actually better than perfect because I got two holes in one, maybe more, so many I'm not even sure. All those important secret meetings at the course meant I couldn't spend as much time as I'd have liked at Mar-a-Lago with the First Lady and her great parents, Viktor and Amalija, who were visiting all weekend. Family, so great, so important, great family.

Mike Pence also happened to be in Palm Beach giving a speech, so I invited him over on Saturday night to take a look at Mar-a-Lago and have dessert with us and then go to wherever he was staying. Mike is doing such a fantastic job as *the* vice president! That's partly because he mostly stays in his office in the West Wing during the day, so he's not in my face all the time getting on my nerves, like certain other members of my team who I can fire anytime I want, and he goes home at a normal time to Karen, who's not only his first wife but is actually *older* than Mike, which is amazing and so great, God bless them. But she's *fifty-eight*. I personally just don't think I could manage to do that. We all have certain lines we can't cross, such as playing with a dog or eating sushi.

At Mar-a-Lago, Mike assured me in private that this thing he said about never being alone with any woman except his wife, even for a meal, was not a hit on me since he'd said it like fifteen years ago—which somebody checked later, and it was true. Nice. Still weird, but nice. Seeing him in Palm Beach, at more of a beautiful *Godfather* kind of place than usual, I realized *he* is probably my Tom Hagen, even looks like Duvall. He might be more loyal to Trump than Bannon. We'll see. I have a feeling I might have a better idea very soon of how much I can trust Steve to get things done that need doing.

★ ★ ★ ★ ★ ★ ★ ★ ★ ★

THE BAD POLLS ARE PROBABLY MOSTLY OR COMPLETELY FAKE

I t's dark.

The only light on in my presidential bedroom in the Washington, D.C., White House is from my phone and the TV.

A week ago the Gallup Poll said most Americans like Trump, which is obviously right. Now they say that 58 percent don't like Trump. A week later? How can that be true? That can't be true. As I warned everybody immediately after my inauguration, negative polls are fake news, the way all the polls were before the election. The press is trying to convince people to turn against me—"Look, he's getting less popular so you should turn against Trump, too!" I think they're also trying to mess with my mind, make me sad. Fortunately I'm extremely, extremely strong. And I do know the bad polls are probably mostly or completely fake.

I told Reince and Jeff Sessions again just yesterday that I wanted to be able to sue the polls and newspapers and fake news shows when they lie about me. Which they're looking into. Like, right now, *Forbes* magazine, who I've been so nice to for so many years, posed for their cover so many times, sold so many magazines for them, I just saw on Twitter they released a new billionaire list. They say I fell from number 205 last year to number 544 now, which is a complete lie.

Fox & Friends just came on. You know, a lot of mornings I feel like Steve Doocy and the guy Brian *really are* my friends. Unlike the dishonest and failing Joe and Mika, who I was so nice to back when they were fair, but, *boom*, I just unfollowed them both on Twitter. It's a privilege, not a right, Joe and Mika.

Rodrigo came in to wake me, but I told him I'd been awake for an hour, working—because writing this book really is important presidential work. *History*.

Like my Fox friend Steve just said on TV, the fake media and Democrats feel better about losing the election if they can say I'm "obsessed" with Obama, using "intelligence" to put surveillance on me during the campaign. I'm not obsessed. Why would I be? I won, nobody disagrees, I won so big, especially in the electoral college, where I won 60 percent of the votes, which is the same as President Reagan and FDR won of the popular vote. The only thing I'm obsessed with is getting the truth out about how Obama and Hillary tried to steal the election by wiretapping me and are now covering it up.

They'll keep the hoax and cover-up going today at Chairman Núñez's House committee hearings, where Comey and the head of the NSA will testify, and I have a very strong hunch they'll both say they have no evidence of Obama's wiretaps on me and that the FBI is investigating "Russia."

Which is going to make me very, very, very angry. I need to get out in front of all that. Hit them before they hit me.

"James Clapper, head of ALL intelligence, above NSA and Comey at FBI, who I could fire, states there is NO EVIDENCE WHATSOEVER POTUS colluded with Russia, where I have no investments and no deals. This story is TOTALLY FAKE NEWS and everyone totally knows it!!!"

Wow. One hundred twenty characters too long. If I ran Twitter I'd make premium memberships so people could write longer ones. No wonder it's not profitable.

Tweak, trim, and . . . *tweet*, wham bam!

Which, by the way, my friend Kanye West told me really is a brilliant line for a song. He's started calling me "Mr. President DJ Trump" when we talk. He said it was okay if I started calling him "my nigga," but we decided I should wait for my second term. Fantastic guy, Kanye.

Feeling better. It's still dark outside.

"The pathetic Democrats who used to beg me for money totally made up the Russian story as their excuse for running Hillary's terrible campaign, worst ever. Gigantic advantage in The Electoral College and STILL COULDN'T BEAT THE UNBEATABLE TRUMP!"

Tweak, trim, *tweet*.

It's still dark. Feeling a lot better. Rodrigo just brought me my bacon, Ovaltine, and supplements and special vitamins.

★ ★

I SHOT OFF ANOTHER TWEET before sunrise about finding the traitors and leakers on "Russia," one more during *Fox &
Friends* about CNN's fake polls, then another during the secret
underground walk to the West Wing about the Clinton campaign's
contacts with Russia. And then while I was watching Comey testify to Núñez on the 65-inch in the room next to the Oval, I did
a tweet about that, like a Trump News bulletin—how the FBI director wouldn't say he *hadn't* told Obama about the wiretapped
calls Flynn made totally without my knowledge to Russia. Wow.

I was glad when Comey announced they were reopening the
investigation of Hillary's dangerous and reckless and criminal
e-mailing the week before the election, last fall—the American
people demanded and deserved that. But since then I've realized
he was actually doing Hillary and the Democrats a big *favor*—
giving them an excuse for losing, which they would have done
anyway. Why did the elite and the press think Comey was so
great in the first place? Because he disobeyed a *Republican* White
House, during Bush. Who appointed Comey? Obama. Who
smiled when he told me not to hire General Flynn, so I'd think
he was joking and hire him anyway? Obama. Who played so
cagey when I phoned him, *twice*, to ask if he was investigating me
and then testified to the committee today, *twice*, that he has "no
information to support those tweets," meaning my tweets about
the wiretaps, calling me, his boss, a liar, and saying the word
"tweets" like they were something dirty? Obama's man Comey.

People say it would look terrible if I fired Comey. We'll see about
that. And that I can't *possibly* go back and replace General McMaster
with General Flynn as national security adviser. We'll see about
that, too. A president can do whatever he wants, even if most of
them have been too scared to use their full powers, like Clark
Kent if he never turned into Superman.

Later in the afternoon I had my first official meeting with my director of national intelligence. "Mike," I said, "how much do we spend on intelligence, total, all in?"

"About eighty billion dollars a year, Mr. President. And it's Dan, sir, not Mike, Dan Coats."

"Right! Right!" Like Mike Pence he's from Indiana, like Pence he also served in Congress, and he could be Mike's brother they look so much alike—plus, my head of the CIA is named Mike, too, Mike Pompei, also was a congressman. It gets confusing. "So, *Dan*, you were in Congress your whole life, good Republican, great Republican, you know how things work, and now you oversee all intelligence for me, including the FBI. I want you to think about how we get Comey to stop wasting time and money investigating the Democrats' fake Russian stories. We all want that, don't we, Dan?" He had some interesting things to say about that—I just "listened" to the "tape" again—but for now I think I'll keep what he said private.

"Different subject. Bigger subject. A plan I was discussing with one of my sons. We're spitballing here, okay?" I didn't tell him I meant my youngest son, because if he knew it was Barron's idea he wouldn't take it seriously. "Let's say we use twenty billion dollars of that eighty to pay twenty thousand a year to a million foreigners all over the world, the *right* million people, what they call 'assets,' they all e-mail us everything they see and hear every week in Kiev or Burma or Africa, all million of them. And then our computers process all those e-mails. That's twenty grand a year on *average*—more in Europe, lots less in Africa, et cetera. Tell me that wouldn't be a much, much better system than we have now! And when we need the rough work done, well, we've got a million guys on retainer to choose from to help out with that."

He nodded and wrote some notes.

"I was talking to one of my senior advisers about this, too, because she was saying her oldest child, the one with the Disney princess name, she's almost six, wants to be a Brownie—a little Girl Scout, not a brownie you eat—but actually, my point is, it made me think of the cookies, when we were young, Dan, remember the cookies? So terrible, *really* bad. And, you know, people send boxes of Girl Scout cookies to the soldiers fighting in wherever, Vietnam, Iran, and the media shows these guys opening them up and crying, and the Girl Scouts think it's because they're so touched, but these guys are actually thinking, 'I'm about to get blown up and my last meal is another box of fucking Thin Mints or Samoas?'—but, anyway, Girl Scout cookies are an *amazing brand*, not good but very successful, and this is my point about our intelligence network, my new idea, because they sell by completely *covering the territory*, right? So we need, like, a worldwide CIA Girl Scout spy network, my million spies. They don't necessarily have to be good, they just have to be *everywhere*."

Dan said it was "a very interesting vision," and he's going to look into it with his experts—the exact same thing he said when I asked him if the CIA killed Kennedy or any other presidents. He said it again a day or two later when I phoned to remind him to help stop Comey's witch hunt. In fact, it's the same answer I got from my White House counsel and Jeff Sessions about suing the fake media for their fake stories. I hear that so much from my people—*We're looking into it, Mr. President.*

I HEAR THAT SO MUCH FROM MY PEOPLE— WE'RE LOOKING INTO IT, MR. PRESIDENT.

By the way, Barron really is the smartest eleven-year-old I've ever met. He just turned eleven, which I remembered even before the Google reminder he set up popped onto my screen, because his birthday is also the first day of spring. For my four previous children, I tried to make sure the birthdays happened in the fourth quarter, calendar year not fiscal year—the later in the year they're born, the better a deal it is for you, since you get the tax deduction for the *whole year* no matter when they're born. My first time out, Don Junior, I hit the bull's-eye—December 31—and I did pretty great with two out of the next three. I love Eric, but Don Junior and I joke about how he always comes close but misses—and after his mother refused to have the C-section on New Year's Eve, he came out right at the beginning of the next calendar year, worst possible timing taxwise. But my reasons for fall and early winter babies weren't just financial—I always preferred to stop "conceiving" during the really hot and sweaty time, late June, July, August, even September. So we never did. I know a lot of people feel the same way.

Where was I?

Right—Obama, the wiretaps. See, I wasn't even thinking about it for like the last ten minutes. Which proves I'm not "obsessed."

In fact, I'm spending all of my time now doing everything I can to help Paul Ryan repeal the terrible, horrible, disgusting, scary, bad, complete, and total out-of-control failure Obamacare, and replacing it with our beautiful new plan. A plan that Ryan, by the way, strongly understands, even though it's all so unbelievably detailed and complicated. It's true that years ago, almost a year ago, at least four months ago, I said that he didn't know how to win and that he's a weak and ineffective leader—and privately I said worse!—but that was before I really got to know Paul.

By the way? One big reason I'm not "obsessed" with the other thing, once and for all proving I'm right about the wiretapping, is because that's about to work itself out in a very interesting way, as Paul Ryan and Steve Bannon both just assured me.

I conserve presidential energy
for important presidential
decision-making duties by riding
in Golf Cart One inside the
White House whenever possible.
The First Lady, who's now 47
(not a typo), prefers to keep
her figure as good as
a 47-year-old woman can.

★ ★ ★ ★ ★ ★ ★ ★ ★

EVERYBODY LIED TO ME

I was so, so excited on Wednesday morning when I saw Congressman Núñez giving his press conferences about the intelligence proving I was right about the wiretaps. I was excited because he was totally vindicating me. The whole thing was going off perfectly. All the shows were showing it, talking about it. "Bombshell," they said.

But I was also excited because—okay, hold on, let me paint the whole picture for you. It's amazing.

We're in the West Wing watching Núñez on TV giving his first press conference over at the Capitol. "There *was* surveillance activity," he says, "it's not right, and the American people shouldn't be comfortable with this." I'm so excited. I almost feel like I need to take one of my other supplements, to calm down. I turn off the TV and sit down with the bureau chief from *Time* magazine, doing an interview for their cover story about how I call out fake news no matter what. I keep telling the guy over and over, "Núñez just gave this incredible press conference, Núñez just gave this fantastic press conference," I even read him a story about it off my phone, "Núñez is now going to the White House to brief Trump."

Then like five minutes later, *boom*, Núñez is here in the West Wing to "brief" me. It's like I read it and then it came true, almost like a piece of magic, when the genie appears to grant your wish.

"Good morning, Mr. President," he said. "I have just received some very important information for you that Speaker Ryan believes you should definitely know about as soon as possible. Because it is extremely important."

"I appreciate that very much, Devin," I replied, "since I know you are the chairman of the House Permanent Select Committee on Intelligence, and therefore have access to top-secret information about things the intelligence community does. Please brief me on what you have found."

Blah-blah-blah, he tells me it looks like Obama could have definitely, absolutely had them wiretap me.

"Well, Congressman Núñez," I told him, "that is very, very important and interesting and historic information, also disgusting, so disgusting, which I am pleased you are putting out there, because the American public definitely has a right to know the truth and your committee must investigate it completely right away. Thank you!"

Then he walks outside to talk to all the reporters right outside here — so I'm watching him in real life, maybe 100 feet away, out my window, but I'm also seeing him live on TV, because the TV I'm watching is right next to the window.

It was another one of those truly fantastic moments as president, the best ones, where it's like I'm in a scene from a movie about President Trump—which makes it all so much better and seem so much more real.

I can't tell you how excited I was. I was on top of the world. It was all working.

That was Wednesday. Now it's Saturday, only three days later. And now everything is ruined.

Everything is crap.

Everybody screwed up.

Everybody lied to me.

Right away the leakers leaked that the night before Núñez came out and backed me up, he got a call from somebody at the White House to come to the White House to look at the secret documents, so that twelve hours later he could come back to the White House to "brief" me about the secret documents. And then Núñez immediately caved. Great work, White House chief strategist. Great work, little *Jeopardy!* winner guy, and great work, Mr. Intelligence Committee Chairman with no more future in my Republican Party.

At the same time, Ryan started telling me he doesn't think we should have his part of Congress, the House, vote on our health plan because he would lose, can't get enough Republican votes. The plan's been out there for two weeks! He said it was great! I went to the mat for it! And then at the last minute yesterday, he comes running over to the White House to tell me we'll *definitely* lose.

I watched him walk into the Oval. Ryan is such a gym rat, almost fifty and so skinny. He's the goody-goody kind of Irish kid I always hated—like Comey at the FBI, although I can also imagine Paul swiping money off the collection plates, but both of them are the same kind of Irish priest type you can't really trust. Sometimes I think I was right about Ryan during the campaign, when I was hitting him on the Twitter. He acts so smart, even though he went to some crappy college in the Midwest, not Ivy League, not Wharton, where I graduated.

I was in the presidential chair behind the big desk, Management 101, Ryan and his pal Reince sitting on the other side. Ryan and Reince, Ryan and Reince, Ryan and Reince. They're like two guys who run a bowling alley in Milwaukee.

"So, *Ryance*, you Washington experts screwed up big-league, huh? If we pull the health plan now, I'm going to look weak. Like a guy who can't get it up and keep it in there, pardon my French, which I'm not, by the way, never was, don't have that problem, that's just a comparison. And because we're talking about health issues."

"Well," Ryan said, staring right at me with that I'm-so-concerned face of his, "*you* are *very* disappointing. You don't even know you're a shitty president, so *shitty*, and you just can't do this job, you freaking cocksucker. You really have *no clue* what you're doing, right? You're just a *zero*, some kind of joke. I hate you. You're *afraid*. And you're just . . . *dumb*."

I leaned forward so fast I knocked the glass of Diet Coke onto the floor. (The springs in this chair in the Oval Office are too springy.) "*What* the *hell* did you just say? Say that again?"

Ryan jerked back and looked all frightened and twitchy. So did Reince. "I—I said I know you are very disappointed, but that we don't know how to get two hundred sixteen, Mr. President, those two hundred *sixteen* votes, we just can't do the job with the Freedom Caucus. I said we really have no clue how to do it right now, just zero way forward with some of these folks. Like I said, I hate where we are, but I'm afraid we're just done."

I shook my head slowly and turned away from them and just stared out the window as they got up to leave. Management 101.

Then I swiveled around. My chief of staff was on his hands and knees right by my desk. "For Christ's sake, Reince, you don't need to pick up the goddamn ice cubes."

I'm still not 100 percent sure I didn't hear Ryan right the first time, and that he panicked and *pretended* he hadn't said all those things. Trust me, I know how that goes. But my point now is that if I did hear him wrong the first time, it really shows you what the stress of this job does to you. It has been such a rough few days, so much stress, so tough.

Speaking of gym rats, Jared was in Aspen all week having fun with Ivanka, who looks so fantastic in the ski outfits, always has. Therefore neither of them gave me any help on the health plan or the wiretaps or any of it. Now they're back in Washington but it's Saturday, so I can't even talk to them because of Schmo Robot, the weekly Jewish holiday. And when we do talk tomorrow, I *know* Jared will be thinking "I told you so" about the health plan.

The First Lady went to Mar-a-Lago straight from New York on my jet yesterday, by herself, which she's never done before. She's probably having fun all over Palm Beach because she's suddenly $3 million richer, because my lawyers just got that disgusting British newspaper to settle with her and admit it didn't have the proof she'd done what it said she'd done, which quite frankly made me lose respect for them as reporters.

★ ★

HEADING OUT TO THE COURSE lifted my spirits. Also, my extra-strength supplements. And at least now with the warmer weather, when I'm stuck in Washington on weekends I can golf. By the way, I realized a few years ago that the people who *claim* they're worried about "global warming" are lying, because who doesn't prefer spring and summer to winter, right?

"I've got a question, Anthony," I said to my fantastic African American secret super protection agent from the special service as we drove in my armored limo out to my beautiful club in Virginia. (Where membership includes reciprocal privileges at all other Trump National and International properties, by the way, including the Southern White House itself.) "Why does the ECM Suburban over there look different today?"

"I believe they washed it this morning, Mr. President."

The ECM Suburban is the coolest of the cool black SUVs that always drives near me in the . . . what do you call it? The . . . cavalcade, Macy's Day, convoy, arcade, JFK, mama's motor-car—

> *MITZI: Presidential to-do list*
> *Book fact-check, word for official presidential*
> *car parade.*

Well, ECM stands for electronic countermeasures, so this one SUV has these domes and pipes and antennas on top that suck in all the radio waves and Arabic or whatever and know if terrorists are trying to get Trump with a remote-control bomb or missile. The First Lady really doesn't like me talking to our son about this, but he's as interested as I am.

"So when the alarm goes off in the ECM Suburban that the bad guys are targeting me, remind me how many smoke grenades they fire off?"

Anthony smiles a little, like friends do. "Releases an initial tranche of ten devices, Mr. President. As would this vehicle. Covering our escape from the kill zone."

"Right. Right." I love hearing Anthony say things like that. *Just like in a movie.* "And then we zoom off at like a hundred miles an hour, maybe even in reverse, then the assault team jumps out of its vehicle and pinpoints the bad guys with lasers and infrared and takes them out with like a thousand bullets a second from their machine guns, right? Like the end of *Bonnie and Clyde* times a million, right?"

"That's the plan, more or less, Mr. President."

And the assault team might also accidentally spray some crossfire into one of the press vans, so tragic.

They didn't have any of that high tech back in the JFK days, which is why Harvey, with just a cheap rifle, Harvey . . . the Lucky Rabbit, Oswald Harvey could get the president. Very lucky shot. If he actually shot him, which nobody believes. When I was fifteen, sixteen, a cadet at the military academy, the movie *PT 109* came out, and everybody said that in my uniform, I looked exactly like Kennedy when he was a World War II hero.

Motorcade.

> *MITZI:*
> *Book fact-check, never mind the last one,*
> *cancel, cancel.*

As we passed Langley, CIA headquarters, I made a little hand gesture I now always do every time I drive back and forth to Trump National, but covering my one finger with the other hand, so nobody can take my picture through the window from a drone or whatever. It always makes Anthony smile.

"If we suddenly came to a CIA roadblock right here, or an FBI roadblock, and a CIA or FBI guy was about to assassinate me, like they did JFK, you'd stop either one of them, right, even though you all work for the government?"

"By any means necessary, Mr. President," which is what he said the other times I asked him the same question.

"Anthony, tell me about your friend in the New York office, the tall guy who's in the First Lady's detail all the time, the one who looks like Robert Pattinson? Jokes around with her in German?"

Anthony didn't flinch. But he's trained not to show any emotion. "Agent Wilson? Excellent man, sir. Straight arrow. We trained together in Georgia."

I had *thought* the word "trained," then Anthony right away said "trained." Wow. Maybe he can do Bannon's mind-reading trick. Or maybe they have a secret technology, another ECM thing, and the information comes through his earpiece.

"He's married?"

"No, sir, Wilson is single."

"Huh. Gay?"

"No, sir."

"Do you know what I'm thinking right now?"

"No, Mr. President."

"Anthony, can I try out your earpiece?"

"Afraid not, Mr. President. They'd fire me for that."

The trip to the golf course from the White House takes forty-five minutes. Marine One could get me there in ten minutes, but Ivanka and everybody says that would look bad. My son Barron gave me a fantastic idea on the phone this morning. He knows all about boats from the Internet. He says a good speedboat, 90 miles an hour, could make the trip from D.C. straight up the Potomac to Trump National—which is right on the river, amazing views—could get me there in *fifteen minutes*, Barron did the math. And one of the really superfast boats, which he says go 300 miles an hour, which a president should really have anyway, could do the trip in *five minutes*. Visionary, right?

WHEN I MENTIONED TO MIKE PENCE RECENTLY HOW GOOD MY GOLF SCORES HAVE BEEN, SO INCREDIBLY GOOD, BETTER THAN EVER, HE SAID "GOOD *PLAYING* COMES FROM GOOD *PRAYING*."

It was 75 degrees when I teed off, sunny, perfect day, somebody said the nicest early spring day in Washington *ever*. It was like I *wished* for great golfing weather so hard I made it happen. When I mentioned to Mike Pence recently how good my golf scores have been, so incredibly good, better than ever, he said "good *playing* comes from good *praying*," and that God wants Trump to succeed—that God actually sent some kind of message to *the* vice president that I would succeed. Well, after this terrible week when so many people failed me, I only shot two holes in one, one each on the front nine and back nine, but every other hole was a birdie or an eagle—meaning I scored my personal best, a *forty-eight*. I could barely believe it myself. I told Anthony to keep the news to himself for the time being, because the media would go crazy, we don't want the distraction, the crews from *Ripley's Believe It or Not!* or whatever. Maybe we'll announce it in the summer, when there's nothing serious going on, do a big ESPN special or something.

HOLE	1	2	3	4	5	6	7	8	9	OUT	INT	10	11	12	13	14	15	16	17	18	IN	TOT	HCP	NET
BLACK	422	578	422	216	491	649	251	448	402	3879		465	168	440	629	230	378	345	546	451	3652	7531		
GOLD	373	523	365	176	388	569	215	431	361	3401		433	150	396	542	173	348	312	502	406	3262	6663		
BLUE	349	510	345	157	365	545	194	374	345	3184		389	133	375	494	157	336	296	484	391	3055	6239		
WHITE	340	451	306	138	299	474	173	288	310	2779		360	122	308	428	150	257	291	448	369	2733	5512		
HANDICAP	15	3	9	17	1	11	13	7	5			6	14	2	12	16	8	18	10	4				
DONALD	3	1	2	4	3	3	3	1	3	23		2	2	3	3	1	3	2	3	3	22	45		
WILBUR	4	5	6	3	5	5	6	3	5	42		5	6	5	4	5	5	4	5	5	44	86		
DMITRY	6	6	4	5	4	6	5	5	6	47		5	6	5	6	4	6	6	6	6	50	97		
PAR	4	5	4	3	4	5	3	4	4	36		4	3	4	5	3	4	4	5	4	36	72		
RED	269	442	257	108	295	430	136	284	274	2495		289	88	302	423	108	254	213	390	344	2411	4906		
HANDICAP	13	1	9	17	7	3	15	11	5			8	14	10	4	16	12	18	6	2				

SCORER: _____   ATTEST: _____ DATE: _____

© Golf ScoreCards, Inc. 03/2014 1-800-238-7287

The actual historic scorecard for a round (and important high-level meeting) at one of my fantastic Trump National Golf Club courses.

When I finished, I walked off the eighteenth green away from the clubhouse, toward the Potomac. Anthony asked where I was going, I told him to radio the speedboat to bring it around for the trip back to the White House. He chuckled, thought I was joking—which then it turned out I was, kind of, I realized. "Ha ha ha," I laughed. "Visionary stuff, seeing the future."

Ivanka can't attend important weekend meetings because of the kosher thing—but out of respect for her and her family, on Saturdays I don't touch anything made in Germany and keep the TV turned way down, so low I can barely hear it.

163

★ ★ ★ ★ ★ ★ ★ ★ ★

IVANKA HAS SUCH A GORGEOUS SMILE

I vanka invited me over to their house for dinner again tonight. "Do I have to eat the 'special food'?" She promised to order in shrimp cocktail and meat loaf from Trump International for me. When I told her I was bringing along my fantastic Oval Office PR girl Hopester as my "date," Ivanka said family only. I figured she wanted me to spend time with the kids, who I love, even though I don't think it's appropriate for them to call me "grandpa." So when I arrived, I was surprised that none of the kids were around.

Ivanka took my left hand in both of hers and brought her face very close to mine. I was holding my breath because I hadn't had an Altoid for a couple of hours, but I always melt when she does that. It was like when I was divorcing her mom and she told me that even though Don Junior hadn't talked to me for like a year, she still loved me—or the way she did a few years later, at fifteen or so, telling me she was only crying because she was so happy I was divorcing her first stepmom.

"We needed to have a meeting alone, Dad, away from the White House."

I looked over at Jared, who wasn't smiling. In fact, he didn't even look like himself. In fact, I didn't recognize him, maybe because he wasn't wearing his tie — and then for a split second I thought he was this popular and goody-goody senior cadet at the New York Military Academy named Bobby, an Eagle Scout, who dressed up as Dracula when I'd just transferred in, Halloween 1959, scared the hell out of me and then broke my pointer finger doing "this little piggy."

Then I realized it wasn't Bobby or Jared, it was one of Ivanka's Secret Service guys. Jared is in Iraq, getting so much media coverage, which really shows you how dumb the media is as well as unfair and dishonest.

"We need to really *talk*, Dad," Ivanka said. She was still holding my hand. "Seriously talk."

I thought she was going to tell me somebody had cancer.

"Is this about Melania getting 'lost' at the White House the other night?" The First Lady flew down from New York for one night to be "First Lady" at a big formal dinner with the senators, and the Secret Service had to go search for her.

"No, Dad, it's about the presidency. Making America great. Making you greater."

This again. First it was the stuff she and Jared always say about my tweets: how they wished I would let her or Hope or somebody in "comms" or one of the lawyers in Don McGahn's office screen them. And how I shouldn't do them first thing in the morning until after I've taken all my supplements and special vitamins.

I did beam out some very strong tweets again this last week, especially yesterday morning, like when I asked why Hillary hadn't apologized for getting all the CNN debate answers in advance from the black Democrat woman with the purple hair. Ivanka said it happened more than a year ago, and it was only a town hall with Bernie Sanders, and only one question.

"Don't be naughty," I told her, "and trust me—I know exactly what I'm doing."

One long tweet this week I didn't trim at all, just split it up, the one where I ordered my House Intelligence Committee to investigate the Clintons' crooked deal with Big Uranium and Russia, plus the 20 million rubles Bill got for a speech in Russia, plus Hillary's dopey and weak "reset" with Russia, plus all of Hillary's praise of Russia, and the shady company Hillary's campaign manager owns in Russia—because the "Russia story" about Trump is all a total disgusting hoax.

"By the way," I said, "I phoned Comey at the FBI again, told him I couldn't get anything done unless he 'lifted the cloud' of the Russia stuff—your fancy phrase, baby."

"That's fine, but when you tweet and talk in public about Russia," she replied, "it just feeds the story, keeps it going."

"That's what you and your smart husband said six years ago about Obama's birth certificate! And I didn't listen to you, and that's why I'm president of the United States and you're a special assistant to the president of the United States and you're married to the senior adviser to the president of the United States! And The Trump Organization, from what I understand, from what a lot of people are saying and I hear everybody is talking about, isn't getting hurt by having the chairman and president—the former chairman and president—being president of the United States." Saying all of that tired me out. But in the movie it will make a fantastic scene.

> *MITZI: Presidential to-do list*
> *Vince Vaughn—has he ever played a blond character?*

Ivanka also said she and Jared *really* didn't understand why I tweeted that Mike Flynn should ask for immunity. "Trust me, Vanksy," I told her. "You don't want to know, okay? But *I* know how the law works and how politicians work, and I know Mike Flynn—know how his mind works, I mean, since I actually barely know him as a person at all, or his business dealings or any of that. But I know what I'm doing."

Besides, I explained *again*, the tweets she and Jared and the First Lady don't like are the ones the *people* like the best and retweet twenty-five thousand times! The highest-rated one so far was when I attacked the judges on their proterrorist ruling, and the first runner-up was calling the news media the enemy of the people! "Baby," I told her, "I really need to keep beaming my truth straight to the people. It's what makes me feel *real*. Also, your little brother says that a Trump army of like twenty-five thousand people would be enough to do whatever we need doing in an emergency, if that ever happened, God forbid."

"Eric said that?"

"No, Barron. He's studied how it worked in other countries. In history. Such an amazing kid. Rodrigo agrees, too. Like a special presidential militia. Just in case. They've got it all figured out."

She said something about how I was sounding like Steve Bannon, that Steve was looking even worse lately even though he started wearing a tie to please me, how Steve really didn't help out on the Obama wiretap business—made it worse—how much Mad Dog doesn't like Steve, he's not a team player, we barely know him, again with how Steve told Jared he was a "cuck" (which actually made me smile), et cetera.

> *MITZI: Presidential to-do list*
> *Song, "BEAMING MY TRUTH STRAIGHT TO THE*
> *PEOPLE / WHAT MAKES ME FEEL REAL," © 2017*
> *by Donald J. Trump.*

"Rodrigo actually agrees with you about Bannon," I said. "I'd asked him how he thought Steve was doing, and he told me he'd heard he wants China and the Philippines to go to war in the South China Sea, which worries Rodrigo. And did you even know that, by the way—China versus the Philippines? Then this morning, out of the blue, Rodrigo shows me another Philippines proverb on his phone, which I had him send to me—*Lahat ng gubat ay may ahas*. It means, 'In every forest, there is a snake.' I felt like I was in a sequel to *Kung Fu*, where Grasshopper's grandson is president and Master Po's grandson works for him. Anyhow, I'm taking Bannon off the VIP list for the National Security Council, okay?"

Ivanka smiled and kissed me on the cheek as she went to get dessert. In private like in public, from behind like from the front, she is the most beautiful special assistant to the president in American history, that I can tell you.

"Hey, Dad," she said when she returned with my Mega Stuf Oreo sundae, "wanna take a couple of fun quizzes? On my iPad?"

"I thought we already figured out what color my aura is. You think maybe it's changed now because I'm president?"

"No, these are different, more like one of those dating quizzes I had you take after Marla left? It's really more of a serious *leadership* quiz."

"Whatever you want."

The first quiz was eighteen statements that I agreed or disagreed with. "'The *Goldberg* Questionnaire,'" I said. "Some professor relative of Jared's?" It had me rate my energy (*highest*) and how much sleep I need (*lowest*), asked if I'm the life of the party (*whenever possible*) and do people have a hard time keeping up with me (*always*), do I come up with so many ideas I jump from one to the other (*yes!*), and do I have special plans for the world (*MAGA!*). The second quiz was similar and longer, forty items, called the NPI. I think I rated myself a five for all of them, I wasn't bragging, just being honest — "assertive," "extraordinary," "special," "born leader," "talent for influencing people," "able to talk my way out of anything," and so forth. When I got to one quiz item, "if I ruled the world it would be a better place," I looked up at Ivanka and smiled.

"Wait a second, Villy Vanka, you're pulling my leg, aren't you? Somebody just made these quizzes up so people could find out how much like *Trump* they are, right?"

"Uh-uh, no, they're actual tests, Daddy, created by professors, been around for years."

"So what's my score?"

"It's more complicated than that. We've found a top expert on success and presidents who gave them to us, she'll score them for you, teaches at Georgetown, lovely woman, Dr. Gloria Müller, ex-military, she's got a security clearance and everything."

"Müller! We love the Germans. Except for Merkel. But what, '*doctor*' like McMaster is a PhD '*doctor*'?" McMaster yaks and yaks in meetings, a lot more than Mike Flynn ever did. Mike was so respectful of the president.

"*Two* PhDs, history, maybe psychology, but an MD, too, got it all, Gloria's amazing, you'll love her—and Dad, I have one more favor. A big one. Jared just called from Iraq and told me that General Dunford just told him—"

"Dunford . . . ?"

"Chairman of the joint chiefs, Irish marine, Boston accent? If you want, they're ready to shoot some cruise missiles at Syria to punish them for the gas attack this morning, teach them a lesson. Then you announce, 'My view of al-Assad has changed since seeing those horrible pictures.'" She took my hand again. "*Please*, Daddy?"

I'm pretty sure her eyes were watering.

"It would make me really happy," she said. "And make you look *very strong* and presidential."

"Sounds good, honey. McMaster mentioned the missiles to me this afternoon, 'option on the table,' or Mad Dog, one of them. But sure, you got it."

"Ooh, great! It'll also be a *fantastic* way to take some air out of the Russia story."

"Which is a hoax anyway, right?"

She smiled. Ivanka has such a gorgeous smile. Unlike me, she enjoys showing her teeth.

★ ★ ★ ★ ★ ★ ★ ★ ★

THE PRESIDENCY REALLY IS LIKE A TV SERIES

I had an unbelievably great, great weekend at the Southern White House, a really outstanding, fantastic, tremendously successful weekend, maybe the best of my presidency, although I've already had so many bests.

First of all, I got three nights and three days down there, which always makes me an even more effective president. Plus two rounds of eighteen at my Trump International—still playing better than I've ever played in my life, such good scores and so many holes in one I'm almost embarrassed to keep telling you about them, like I'm bragging, so I'll just say—I'm pretty sure one of my scores was literally better than anyone has played, anyone, ever. I swear. But now I promise not to mention my scores again. Until we do the ESPN special, which Ivanka and Jared think should wait until 2018, after the midterm election, a Thanksgiving special, which is a great idea.

Second of all, she was so right about shooting the cruise missiles into Syria, the Tomahawks, which I did as soon as I landed in Palm Beach—"We're locked and loaded, sir!" Mad Dog actually said, which was so fantastic, and "Fire away!" I then commanded— the media and all the globalists were all "Oh, now he's a major, major president, so strong, not like Obama, Russia criticized him, which means he's not a puppet!" So easy. I said to my team at Mar-a-Lago on Friday—Bannon, Jared, Reince, Tillerson, McMaster—I told them: "This is what I've been saying, the presidency really is like a TV series, okay, each season you need certain big moments, and we have to do something like the cruise missiles once a season, okay?" I think they get it now. And nobody died, which is also great, almost nobody, very few, they say rounded off it's actually zero.

By the way, I've also been good lately about not beaming too many tweets Ivanka and Jared don't like.*

Third of all, thanks to me, after my long weekend in Palm Beach with President Xi, which by the way you pronounce like you pronounce *Zsa Zsa*, America now has a relationship with China the likes of which we've literally never had ever before.

"Wow, President Xi," I said when he arrived at Mar-a-Lago, "what're you, six feet? So tall! Very tall! Most Chinamen not so tall! Good for leader to be tall!" He appreciated the compliment, and that I was speaking clearly, since he doesn't really speak English. "Sorry you had to *drive* from airport," I said, making a steering wheel motion with my hands, very diplomatic. "Next time take *chopper* directly—best helipad under construction, right there, on lawn." The two of us had great chemistry immediately.

---

*Barron showed me how to save the tweets I write but don't beam immediately so I can dig them out later if I want, such as this one I didn't send: "If goofy old Elizabeth Warren were president she would never let the generals send in the Tomahawks—even though she'd be POTUS POCAHANTAS!!!" Great, right?

Because North Korea had just fired a missile, like they did when the Japanese prime minister was visiting, and we were at Mar-a-Lago, just like with Abe, it was a crazy déjà vu thing, so at first I mixed up the two leaders a little—mentioned sushi and the yakuza to President Xi, forgot for a second he already *does* have nuclear. So actually it turned out to be a good thing that Xi doesn't golf, because I could use that to keep straight which was which. I also used *China big, Japan small*, because Abe was the normal Asian miniheight. (Xi told me Kim Jong-un is a little guy, too. So I've just ordered the National Security Council to make me this fantastic chart, like a brochure, that has pictures of every world leader arranged from tallest to shortest. I think it'll come in very handy. When you see *all* of them on the master chart, it's amazing *how many* aren't white. Which is fine.)

Xi's First Lady, Madame Peng, is actually a very good-looking woman— I'm serious, especially for her age, reminded me of Imelda Marcos, who by the way once tried to pick me up at Studio 54 when her husband was president of the Philippines.

> *MITZI: Presidential to-do list*
> *Tell Rodrigo and President*
> *Duty-Free about Imelda.*

WORLD LEADERS BY HEIGHT

6'2"
PRESIDENT TRUMP
United States

6'2"
JUSTIN TRUDEAU
Canada

6'2"
BASHAR AL-ASSAD
Syria

6'
BENJAMIN NETANYAHU
Israel

5'10"
MALCOLM TURNBULL
Australia

5'9"
EMMANUEL MACRON
France

5'9"
SHINZŌ ABE
Japan

5'8"
ENRIQUE PEÑA NIETO
Mexico

5'8"
THERESA MAY
United Kingdom

5'7"
KIM JONG-UN
North Korea

5'6"
VLADIMIR PUTIN
Russia

5'6"
MOON JAE-IN
South Korea

5'5"
ANGELA MERKEL
Germany

Madame Peng was one of the biggest celebrities in Chinese entertainment before Xi was even president, which means we have a
lot in common. Although, it turned out, she wasn't related to my
friend Mr. Peng, the chef who invented General Tso's chicken and
when I was young operated a very nice restaurant, Uncle Peng's,
right near the UN, where I built my fantastic Trump World Tower.
In fact, Madame Peng never even heard of General Tso's chicken,
and says she never met Ivanka's friend Wendi Deng, Rupert's
ex, which also surprised me, so my joke about Wendi Murdoch
dating Putin didn't really land. She did giggle when I told her
that her husband looks exactly like my regular waiter at Uncle
Peng's, Lew or Lou or Lu, great guy who'd lost half his thumb
and index finger from a cherry bomb, because the Chinese really
are completely crazy about fireworks. During dinner one night at
Mar-a-Lago, Madame Peng mentioned their daughter just graduated from Harvard, and since Jared was right across from us, I
joked that at least she and President Xi probably didn't have to
spend $2.5 million to get her into Harvard like the Kushners did!
We had a truly great chemistry.

During the day, between my golf games and the dinners, I had
fantastic conversations with President Xi about Korea, totally
opened our kimonos. (Which Tillerson later said I probably
shouldn't have said, that term, but whatever, I'm not PC.) What I
thought before we talked was that North Korea was their Puerto
Rico, if Puerto Rico had its own nuclear; a poor, rough little place
over to the side that he runs. I was somewhat wrong—and I do
admit it when I'm somewhat wrong. Anyhow, President Xi is going
to take care of North Korea for us now, and we're good on the big
trade deficits and everything else, maybe in the future America
won't keep so much military in South Korea, who knows. But here's
the thing: I've never been to North Korea, never read a book about
it, never took a course on it, none of that, but now, by discussing
it strongly for ten minutes with the *real* expert with the real
power, not some CIA "analyst" or State Department know-it-all, I

now totally, completely, absolutely understand. I guess it's like with the special tutors who helped get my kids into good colleges. That's efficiency, that's Management 101, that's how CEOs do it, and it's how President Trump does the presidency.

Everybody for the last two weeks has been all, "Oh my God, Trump's going to attack North Korea, oh my God, he's gonna start a war, oh no." But I had several great follow-up phone calls from my very close friend Xi, who respects me in a way he never respected Obama—that I can tell you, trust me. He reminded me that Kim just wants to feel good about himself—nobody likes being called unbalanced or overweight or spoiled. Especially if you're powerful and rich but all isolated from the world like Mr. Kim is, right? Trump understands how to flatter people. Negotiation 101.

★ ★

IN ADDITION TO PROTECTING AMERICA and keeping the peace, as president you still have to take care of little things. Like when after we spanked Assad and Sean got into so much trouble with the rude, mean media for saying even Hitler didn't gas his people like Assad does. When he was apologizing to me in the Oval afterward, he told me he thought "holocaust center" was a more dignified way to say it than "concentration camp," which is actually true, and then Sean cried a little, which I must tell you docs make a big impression on me, like people who can speak foreign languages or when women have their periods. So in my regular call with Rupert the next day, after I thanked him for getting rid of the *Wall Street Journal*'s one columnist who hates me, I asked if he'd give poor little Sean a phone call to buck him up, and he did. Management 101.

That was right before Ivanka's special Georgetown leadership scientist, Dr. Müller, came in for our first briefing. Such a smart lady, Yale, U.S. Navy intelligence four years, very knowledge-able about what presidents go through, and extremely good-looking, a little younger than the First Lady, like Kelly McGillis when she played Tom Cruise's girlfriend in *Top Gun*, "Charlie" the Air Force "scientist."

She said what Ivanka told me was true — that because she's tech-nically a doctor, everything I say to her is private, if I want, like with a lawyer, patient-attorney privilege. She said my scores on the leadership tests, she called them "inventories," were "really exceptional" and "almost literally off the charts." Which I thought she might have been saying just to get on my good side, but she didn't say it with a smile, she said it in this serious and neutral and kind of mysterious way, the way the First Lady talks a lot in private. Then Dr. Müller showed me the graphs and I saw it was totally true on both, the Goldberg and especially the NPI, my scores on both were so high, so amazing. Although I wasn't surprised.

She asked if any of the presidential duties made me tense, or if I ever doubted my "abilities." *Very flirty*, I was thinking.

"Well, Charlie," I said, "may I call you Charlie? I never doubt my abilities, *never*, because in the long run I *always* succeed, so don't worry about that. It's *all* tense, winning requires tense. Forget 'tense,' what I really wish, between you and me, is that I didn't find so much of being president so *boring*. And not *just* boring — I mean, lots of things are boring, like the news on PBS, which I turned to by mistake last night,

> **I NEVER DOUBT MY ABILITIES, *NEVER*, BECAUSE IN THE LONG RUN I *ALWAYS* SUCCEED, SO DON'T WORRY ABOUT THAT.**

even though it was pretty nice to me. And most people are bor-ing, like I know people who even say their daughters-in-law and even some of their children are boring. But so much of being president is complicated *and* boring. Like instructions on appliances, or filling out your own tax returns, or college."

When she asked how I "relieved the tension," I really wondered if she was sliding into Monica Lewinsky territory, but she meant religion, hobbies, exercise, et cetera. "All of the above," I said. I told her I play two rounds of golf twice a week while I'm having presidential meetings, "multitasking," went to church in Palm Beach on Easter, very nice, and my new hobby is music, writing songs, great songs, platinum records.

I also told her my best tweets relieve a lot of the tension. "But they don't *want* me to do those tweets, Ivanka and Jared and all of them. The boring tweets they have me do feel like . . . nothing. I go for a few days, sometimes almost a week, and then I just have to blast out some real ones, you know? I feel penned up."

"Pent up?"

"*Penned*, like an animal, you know, like the pigs on the farm next to Trump Turnberry, my fantastic golfing resort in Scotland. And I feel more penned up when I'm at the White House, which I don't own, just like I don't own that Scottish bastard's pig farm, pardon my French. Firing those missiles at Syria felt like the greatest tweet ever, like a tough and important message that made *everybody* go *whoa*, he's the *president*, he's the man, America first. I guess that's how a lot of presidents do relieve tension. And I did it from the Southern White House, so I felt very, very relaxed afterward." So then I guess I understood what Dr. Müller had been getting at—tweeting and firing missiles and having sex are all very different things, but afterward you're relaxed in a similar way. Smart lady.

She said what she's learned as a historian, studying leaders, is that what the greatest ones do is figure out who around them they *trust* the most and "invest even more" in those trustworthy people.

"Wow," I said, "no wonder Ivanka likes you—you sound just like her!"

I totally trust Ivanka. I don't not trust Jared, and he can be very annoying, and he's too skinny for a man, but I trust him, the way I trust Rodrigo and Anthony, the way you trust trustworthy people who don't contain Trump genes.

Dr. Müller also said that if I feel anxious around Bannon, or I have a feeling he's reading my thoughts, I probably ought to spend less time with him. Which got me thinking—that when he finally leaves the White House, and if he returns to entertainment, I could let him develop my *President Batman* and *Kung Fu President* ideas as movies or shows, and use my songs on the soundtracks. When I said that, Dr. Müller gave me two thumbs-up, which was nice, very cute, since that's a Trump thing.

> *MITZI: Presidential to-do list*
> *Rodrigo, pharmacy, pick up new Dr. Müller*
> *supplements and vitamins.*

And speaking of "multitask," I just wrote half a chapter of this book by talking to a professor for an hour, the way I used to talk to the "writers" of my earlier books, but this time I'm totally in charge of what gets written, it's *really me*, and I keep the total advance and all the royalties. Win-win.

★ ★ ★ ★ ★ ★ ★ ★ ★

I NEVER PANIC

A s Rodrigo brought in my breakfast, he was shaking his head. I thought it was still because he was upset about what happened last night when Ted Nugent and Kid Rock and Sarah Palin came over for dinner—the mooning on the Truman Balcony, the fingering the baked Alaska, the two missing saucers, et cetera.

He was still shaking his head as he picked up the empty Doritos bags and Diet Coke cans from my bedside table.

I looked at the Filipino proverb on my breakfast tray, which he now includes every week or so, in the language the natives there call "Tag Along" and also in actual English. *A sleeping shrimp is carried away by the current.*

"Are you saying I should get out of bed, Rodrigo?"

"No—but I saw on Fox News that you have been fired as president, my friend, oh, really sad, because of what those women said in the *New York Times* about sex."

I was so surprised that Ovaltine and bacon bits sprayed out my nose all over my newspapers. "You mean *Bill O'Reilly*, Rodrigo—nobody fired *me*, nobody *can* fire me."

"Yes, of course, Mr. President, that's what I said—I'm sad for your friend Mr. O'Reilly, because he's out at Fox News."

Bill was actually more of a colleague than a friend, like Stone Cold Steve Austin and Hulk Hogan weren't really "friends." But for the elitists and liberals and fake media, getting O'Reilly was like a dress rehearsal for getting *me*—"We can't destroy Trump, so we'll destroy the next best," a tall guy in his sixties on Fox all the time, a well-known guy from the New York suburbs but so successful in Manhattan the Manhattanites hate him, a contro-versial guy with a sense of fun who doesn't put up with PC and always calls a spade a spade, almost never literally. They were all fantasizing about whacking me when they whacked him, that I can tell you, 100 percent. Last night when I heard the news about O'Reilly, it did make me call down to the Secret Service and tell them we needed to permanently close the sidewalk outside the White House for security reasons, and I did get short of breath for a couple of minutes, although the White House chief usher was wrong and inappropriate when she very loudly said she was sure "the president seems to be having a *panic attack*."

I don't panic. I never panic. I didn't panic from 1990 to 1992 when I did not go bankrupt. Ask any member of my family, any-body who knows me or ever worked for me. "Trump does not panic," every one of them will tell you, I promise. Anybody who ever might have seen me panic, such as when I was little, is dead now—such as my father, who died on a fantastic summer Friday a week after my birthday in 1999, when I was single, such a great time in my life, although "bittersweet" because of the funeral, although he was extremely old and totally out of it by that time. Instead of panicking, I always eliminate the problems that are trying to make me panic.

I'm not panicking now. It wasn't panicking to change my mind about China or Syria or NATO or being nice to North Korea or anything else. In fact, I didn't really change my mind at all, now I can reveal that—my current positions were always my true positions, but winners don't show their cards, winners are unpredictable, winners keep the losers off guard. Also, it's like on every season of *The Apprentice* and *The Celebrity Apprentice* and in all movies—to keep people interested you need what they call "an arc," with the hero doing surprising things and going through plot twists. Entertainment 101, which is really just a different name for Leadership 101 and Marketing 101.

I'm not panicking about the Russia hoax or about the disgusting "intelligence" leaks or about the fake polls. I'm not panicking about Mike Flynn betraying me, because he knows loyalty, and the section of the Constitution that lets the president pardon anybody for anything, which is amazing, and why I sent Mike a message today—"Stay strong, you'll be fine, promise." And I'm not panicking about the dishonest fake media and archaic rules in Congress and all the so-called judges and pathetic Democrats and bureaucrats in the "deep state"—which, like most people, I'd never even heard of until now, so scary—all of them "colluding" to stop me from making America great.* I don't believe they all

---

*By the way, speaking of so-called judges, remember how I said at the very start, many chapters ago, how I told my White House counsel I wanted the unfair "Mexican-American" Judge Curiel from my Trump University case to get one of the cases of the deported illegals, to show how the system is rigged against me? He did! Why? Because I wished so hard for it to happen! Call it prayer, call it one of Trump's special powers, call it whatever you want, but it's true.

hate America, the way Bannon thinks, because many of them are really just like Ivanka but without money or nice clothes or Trump genes, but they *do* all hate the idea that I'll succeed, so they're willing to keep America in terrible, terrible shape so that Trump looks worse. But I *will* win, I will *win*, *I* will win—or as my dad used to say so loud the neighbors could sometimes hear, "*Sieg ist mein*," which means the same thing.

My amazing son Barron just put a countdown clock on my phone, a "widget" he calls it, that shows me all the time how many days I have left in my first one hundred days—I'm down to nine.

I'm not panicking—I'm *focusing*. Very, very different. If you panic it means you're scared. When I need something important to happen quickly, I command, I make demands, I make *other* people panic if necessary, make *them* scared, the people who work for me and the people against me, so then they do whatever has to be done—and therefore Trump doesn't need to feel scared or humiliated. And the people around me will always feel much more scared and humiliated than I ever will, which is actually the next best thing to never feeling it yourself at all. Management 101 and Leadership 101. ME-dership 101!

> *MITZI: Presidential to-do list*
> *Song, "I DON'T PANIC / I COMMAND, I MAKE*
> *DEMANDS / MAKE OTHER PEOPLE SCARED /*
> *ME-DERSHIP 101," © 2017 by Donald J. Trump.*

> *MITZI: Presidential to-do list*
> *Invite Kanye to Southern White House to discuss*
> *Trump rap album, advance warning for club members.*

Focus is why Jared and other people have been very nicely offering to stop a terrible *Enquirer* story about Joe and Mika if they'll publicly apologize to us.

Focus is getting Obamacare repealed now and replaced by whatever. "You're not 'moving on' from repealing and replacing,"
I told Ryan and Priebus. "You've got nine days, two weeks tops—
or else, *Reincey*." Which scared him, but I noticed actually made
Ryan smile.

Focus is why I told my financial and economic guys *weeks ago*
we need to announce our fantastic tax plan before the hundred
days are up, biggest tax cut in the history of this country and
one of the biggest ever anywhere in the world—almost *no* taxes.
What the plan *has* to do, right away, I told them, is get rid of all
the taxes that are there only to hurt the successful people—the
"alternative" tax, the terrible new tax on stock market winners
that pays for collapsing Obamacare, the tax that takes away the
money you want to leave to your kids when you pass away,
et cetera. I have another idea, which my financial guys are too
scared to propose this time around. After any American is murdered by an illegal immigrant or a terrorist, the victim's family
would never have to pay taxes of any kind again. Even sales tax,
because we'd issue cards that say TAX AMNESTY: ILLEGAL IMMIGRANT
MURDERER VICTIM, which they'd present at the cash registers, or
enter a code if they shop online, although in any case, no more
taxes, ever. But even before we do that, our tax and economic
plan is going to make America like it was when everybody
lived in nice homes and almost nobody got murdered and the
dads who didn't do the dirty work always wore ties. But our plan
will *also* make America like you've never seen it before, like on
The Jetsons.

★ ★

AFTER I ANNOUNCED we were about to announce the amazing tax plan, my financial and economic guys claimed to my face
that I'd never told them about the hundred-days deadline—which
is *so not true* that I laughed as hard and long as I'd laughed since

one of Tillerson's people mentioned a real African president named "Omar Bongo." My economic guys got the message and while I was still laughing rushed out of the Oval and got right to work on it, since they knew they'd screwed up. They finished the plan in a few days, which is all they needed—as anybody who's ever paid for a term paper the night before it's due knows.

The rush also made it more *exciting* for everybody. We were ending our show's first season, one hundred days, thirteen weeks, and excitement is so important in any finale episode—like on Day Ninety-Seven when I said I was going to pull out of the Clintons' disastrous trade deal with the Mexicans and the Canadians, which everyone knows destroyed our economy. *"No more NAFTA"*—and everybody got excited! Ivanka said she had a strong feeling the president of Canada and the prime minister of Mexico would both call me the next day literally begging to make a better deal—and *that's exactly what happened*, boom, boom, one right after the other! (I'm glad to know now that Ivanka inherited some of my "special" mental powers. I think Barron is developing them, too. On Easter Sunday I was kind of talking in my mind about North Korea's nuclear to my brilliant MIT uncle, Professor John Trump, who died right before my first appearance on *60 Minutes*, before I was forty, so sad. Suddenly Barron says that I'm like Professor X, the star of *X-Men*—or Professor X and Magneto combined, which Barron says would be the best. I need Barron around more. So smart.) Anyhow, on Day Ninety-Eight, Trudeau and Piñata both called and caved and said they'd change NAFTA to make America first.

On Day Ninety-Nine I realized we'd done nothing at all on one of my very important promises during the campaign—that we would sue all of the lying women who lied that I "assaulted" them. Unfortunately I can't do this by an executive order, because what didn't happen didn't happen when I was a private citizen, which also means I can't use my White House counsel or the

Secret Service or FBI on it. Ivanka *begged* me to wait until 2018 to announce it, but I told my personal lawyers to start all the background work, investigating if it was Hillary or Obama or both who hired those disgusting women to come forward and tell their lies. By the way, I've never "sexually assaulted" *any* woman in my entire life. Sure, once they give me the sign, I'm no sissy, because, quite frankly, most women want that Robert Mitchum–Jim Brown type of man, which is a major reason I've always done so well with the ladies. But according to the women I know, other women these days are being brainwashed by PC to call everything "assault," which is so unfair and disgusting.

On the morning of Day One Hundred, when I got my weekly Filipino proverb along with my bacon and Ovaltine—*Ang umaayaw ay di nagwawagi, ang nagwawagi ay di umaayaw*, which is a lot of words for "Succeed or die"—I decided to call the president of the Philippines, where it was like dinnertime the night before. I love that international time travel thing. To be quite honest, it's military leverage we have over Kim Jong-un if it ever did come to war, a thing that our generals and "intelligence" and other presidents have never realized we could use to our advantage. America First also means *we* get the *days* first, because it's still Friday in Korea when we've already moved on to Saturday in America. Which reminds me of a picture book I had when I was young, *The Relativity Express*, Christmas gift from my MIT genius uncle, Dr. John Trump, about a train that travels so fast it goes back to cowboy times, which gave me the idea in fifth grade of traveling to the early 1900s and buying up certain real estate for nothing because none of the sellers would know their properties were going to become super valuable. After I found out that kind of time travel was impossible, I lost interest in science.

Rodrigo told me that President Duty-Free speaks English, which was great. And it turns out his first name is also Rodrigo, which is spooky, but made me feel like we were friends right away.

Good guy, great guy, wonderful energy—told me his last name is actually Dirty Tea, very polite about that, but that if I ever called him Duty-Free again, he might "mistake" some of our Manila embassy staff for drug dealers. He was joking, and we had a good laugh—but I told him I very seriously loved the fantastic, unbelievable job he was doing with his drug problem and wanted him to teach us how to stop ours. He made shooting sounds, like we did when we were kids—"*Pkew! Pkew! Pkew!*"—which was *very* funny. He also said he hoped I wouldn't start a war with North Korea—or at least let him know in advance so he could get out of the Orient ahead of time! Funny, funny guy. Great chemistry, so I invited him to both White Houses, and told him when he comes my senior steward and special international minority adviser would fix him some bull's penis soup with chicken toenails and crickets—which my Rodrigo swears they actually eat, which does make you wonder.

Around the end of the first one hundred days I also made everybody excited when I said Kim Jong-un is a smart cookie and tough and that I'd be honored to get together with him. Xi said that's how to get him to do what you want, duh, but I also really think Kim *is* a smart, tough young guy. Like the good Arabs, Ahmet Ertegun in Turkey and General Sissy in Egypt, like Putin and Xi. I enjoy these guys because there's no bullshit involved, no fake "principles," it's all totally honest—and unlike the Europeans and the pretty boy gym rats who run Canada and Mexico, they don't try to make it like I'm not as smart or sophisticated or nice as they are. It's related to why I was so attracted to my wives—none of them speak English perfectly, so it was never like they would be judging me.

IT'S RELATED TO WHY I WAS SO ATTRACTED TO MY WIVES—NONE OF THEM SPEAK ENGLISH PERFECTLY, SO IT WAS NEVER LIKE THEY WOULD BE JUDGING ME.

By the way, speaking of not judging, you know who else I've developed great relationships with? The leaders of Africa and South America, who supposedly don't like America. Well, they like *me*, which means they're finally learning to like America. It's been secret until now, Ivanka and Jared made me pinky swear I'd keep it secret, but every month or so I do the FaceTime with Bob Mugabe, who's been head of Zimbabwe for *thirty-seven years*, just about the longest in the world, which is so impressive, and he speaks perfect English. Also Nick Maduro, the head of Venezuela, not such good English, but he sells us oil, *so much* oil, as much oil as Saudi Arabia, which most people don't know, and he also understands Venezuela could be a beautiful resort country again. We have good chemistry, Bob and Nick and I.

Even though the "first one hundred days" thing isn't in the Constitution or the laws or other rule books at all, just a totally meaningless test the fake media fabricated to make Trump panic and feel bad, like it used to do about my fingers and hands, now even the pundits and professors are saying I had the most memorable first one hundred days since FDR—somebody showed me the articles, the headlines. And to celebrate we had a tremendous rally on Day One Hundred in Pennsylvania, where I beat Hillary last fall even though no Republican had ever won Pennsylvania. I felt so great, so phenomenal—and I think the new supplements made my Superman feelings last a lot longer than usual, even though Ivanka, who walked by just now as I was saying this, reminded me to "write" that all my pills and capsules are totally natural and organic vitamin-type things.

When I asked Reince why we hadn't started scheduling two or three rallies a week, like I'd ordered, he claimed he thought I'd said one every two or three weeks. "Two or three every week would be a lot of rallies, Mr. President. An awful lot."

Believe it or not, until now there was never an official American commander in chief uniform! For the time being I only wear it privately—such as here in the Southern White House, doing what Ivanka calls my "mindfulness practice."

"Right? *Right!* Exactly! You saw how happy those people in Pennsylvania were on Saturday, all one hundred thousand of them shouting 'Trump! Trump! Trump!' The people *love* the rallies, Reince. They *need* the rallies." The only problem with Pennsylvania was the Secret Service dogs sniffing for explosives—I actually *saw* them right around my podium. "But as we do more rallies," I reminded Reince, "don't forget the new dog protocols, okay?" The canine teams need to go in and be gone at least twenty-four hours before Trump arrives—and I don't care if that means more uniformed Secret Service overtime. No dogs.

I was on a roll again, so I kept the action going a few days past Day One Hundred, making it all look totally off the cuff, surprise, surprise, surprise, keeping the excitement up—like saying how I might raise the gasoline tax to pay for new everything, highways, bridges, airports, airplanes, ships, missiles, tanks, lasers, computers, the best, all brand-new, and how I might break up JPMorgan Chase and Citigroup and Goldman Sachs and all of the big banks.

And then *right at the end* of the first one hundred days, the very end, Day One Hundred Five, whatever, Ryan and I guess Reince came through in the clinch on repeal and replace, we won, couldn't be done and I did it, back from the dead, we had a beautiful party out in the Rose Garden.

> *MITZI: Presidential to-do list*
> *Song, "REINCE AND RYAN, REPEAL AND REPLACE /*
> *REALLY WON, COULDN'T BE DONE, BACK FROM*
> *THE DEAD / OUT IN THE ROSE GARDEN PARTY*
> *PARTY PARTY," © 2017 by Donald J. Trump.*

I felt so great, so incredible, so amazing, so fantastic, so outstanding, literally unbelievable. So truly, extremely, absolutely, unbelievably, tremendously phenomenal, the best. The best, the best. Just the best.

★ ★ ★ ★ ★ ★ ★ ★ ★

I HAD TO "KILL" HIM— KILL IN QUOTATION MARKS

Like I've said, even though I always kind of forget it myself, big downs follow the big ups. And I'm Trump, so both are bigger than you can probably even imagine.

During the Rose Garden party, I glanced over at Paul Ryan and he looked evil, like a smiling vampire, not like the kid on *The Munsters*, who a lot of people say Paul resembles, but like Barnabas on *Dark Shadows*, actually scary. I reminded myself that Paul always glances at himself in windows and mirrors, which is unvampire, but sort of gay, and people have told me vampires go both ways, biting and sucking men, women, whoever. The First Lady is actually kind of a vampire expert, because vampires originated in her part of the world. In any case, that afternoon Paul Ryan definitely looked untrustworthy, and when I have strong instincts, they always mean something—I trust my gut more than I trust anything, the way other people trust "God" or "science."

I went to the Oval Office to gather my thoughts and take some supplements. When Rodrigo brought me an afternoon tray of chicken tenders from downstairs, it had one of his little cards with the Filipino proverb—it was *Huwag kang magtiwala sa di mo kilal*, "Don't trust strangers," which I strongly agree with, but it's also a Cash-22, because deep down, except for maybe your mother and some of your children, who isn't a stranger?

Rodrigo told me that his boss, the chief usher, had been on his case ever since I made him my senior steward and special international minority adviser. Which made me angry.

"We're gonna do a scene from *The Apprentice*, Rodrigo. Ready . . . roll sound . . . *action!*"

While I ate my chicken tenders, I called Reince, who was still out in the Rose Garden—I could watch him as he saw my call come in and put down his beer and got all nervous, which I enjoyed. I told him to fire the chief usher *now*. Definitely not because she's African American or a woman or the first African American woman in that job, but because her staff, especially her minority staff, has totally lost confidence in her, and also she may be leaking to Obama, Lynch, Holder, et cetera, who knows.

While I was still talking to Reince, a call came in from Jeff Sessions. Jeff did his nervous, stuttery thing. He reminds me of that kid in *To Kill a Mockingbird* who pours pancake syrup all over his food. I liked that kid, even though he was a loser.

> *MITZI:*
> *Pancake syrup boy in* To Kill a Mockingbird,
> *who is that?*

Mitzi didn't understand, or didn't know. Sad. I thought I could totally trust Mitzi.

Anyway, I told Sessions to stop stuttering like a little boy. "Is this about Comey again, his weird stuff in the Senate yesterday, the 'I prayed to find a third door' and 'makes me nauseous' stuff? I've got it cued up on the TiVo here if you want to come over and watch again. Unless you're too *recused*."

He said he was calling about the FBI director, but some new things—Comey just asked for a bigger budget for the FBI to investigate Russia. "And he's been telling people around town that, that—that you're 'abnormal' and 'crazy,' Mr. President."

I thought it might be another one of those mental tricks, where the things people tell me sound worse than they really are, so I had Jeff repeat it, and put him on speaker so Rodrigo could hear, too. "*Yes*, Mr. President," Jeff said, "that's right, Comey wants more money to investigate the campaign's connections to Russia, *and* he's been telling people 'the president is not normal' and 'the president seems crazy.'"

Trump is not normal? I'm one of the *most* normal people you'll ever meet—it's why all the most normal Americans support me so strongly, because I'm just like them, except maybe smarter and a lot more successful, and my wife is much, much better looking. If you're worth $20 billion because you built the most successful business of its kind on earth *and* you get elected president, doesn't that mean you're the *opposite* of "crazy"? I always thought Comey was a freak, way too tall, reminds me of that extremely tall guy who wrote *The Andromeda Strain*, great book, the last "novel" I read, who died very young, like sixty-six. I wonder if maybe Comey has whatever super-tall-man disease he had. In any case, until Sessions told me he's been calling Trump crazy, I'd really never realized he was such a total delusional fruitcake. "Wow," I said.

What was even worse, Rodrigo told me I'd spent seventeen straight nights in the White House, more than ever before in history. I think what I call the "kryptonite" there really was starting to weaken my powers—which, by the way, Rodrigo says might be connected to the lead in the very old White House pipes, like in that hellhole city in Michigan where I campaigned, Fink, Clint, Flynn, that one. I needed to get to a place that I own and totally control. Immediately.

The closest Trump homes to Washington, D.C., are New York—but I knew they may still be wiretapping me at the Northern White House, Trump Tower, one reason I've stayed away, and they'd be *expecting* me to go there. So I outsmarted them, kept them off guard, zigzagged in a fantastic way, totally like a movie, even more so because I played the special soundtrack Barron put on my phone—I went in Air Force One to an airport named after a rich and handsome president with a beautiful First Lady, then a fast Marine One flight, with the decoy Marine Ones around us, which I love, like we're on a combat mission, right into a heliport on Wall Street, and then it was like I'm having a commander in chief ticker-tape parade as we convoy up to the USS *Intrepid*

WE CONVOY UP TO THE USS *INTREPID* ANCHORED IN THE HUDSON RIVER, WHICH IS LIKE MY SPECIAL PRESIDENTIAL AIRCRAFT CARRIER KEEPING NEW YORKERS FROM ATTACKING ME.

anchored in the Hudson River, which is like my special presidential aircraft carrier keeping New Yorkers from attacking me, then after dark we chopper out to the Trump National Golf Club in New Jersey, to my private villa that I *own*, on 525 acres which I also own. Anthony told me it's the Trump property with the most defensible terrain and best weapons-system positions—and the clubhouse, open for me around the clock, has the fantastic fried mac 'n' cheese bites.

★ ★ ★ ★ ★ ★ ★ ★ ★ ★ ★ ★ ★ ★ ★ ★ ★ ★ ★ ★

THE MAC 'N' CHEESE BITES WERE FANTASTIC, but all weekend I was cooped up with the First Lady and three of my grandchildren, and it was too cold to golf. Watching the news shows Sunday morning with Ivanka and Jared was horrible. It was suddenly like everything on TV was one big Internet video jiffy looping over and over, Hillary and Comey, Comey and Hillary, Hillary and Comey, over and over on every channel all at once, even Fox News. Hillary saying Comey won the election for Trump, Comey saying Trump made him nauseous during the election . . . and then the French woman, Le Pen, Marine One, she lost, she loses big-league, and even though it could have been rigged, everybody on TV saying it's bad for Trump, the French rejected Trump, Putin likes her and she's a loser so Trump is now a loser.

I realized I had no choice. Comey was a major, major enemy, and I had to "kill" him—kill in quotation marks, the kind of quotation marks I put around "wiretap," the kind that mean you're being sarcastic but still serious. I talked to my top team, even *the* vice president, and they were all for it—Ivanka pointed out it was like a perfect random sample of Americans confirming my judgment: Mike Pence the Midwestern evangelical, Don McGahn the tough Irish New Jersey lawyer, Jared the smooth Jewish Ivy League media guy, my private personal Trump security chief Keith. It was like *The A-Team*, and then when Rodrigo said he agreed I should can Comey—he repeated his proverb about a snake in every forest—I even had my Mr. T! Reince was kind of a nervous Nelly, but I got him to go along when I said, "Fee-fi-fo-fum, *somebody's* gonna get fired this week," which was another example of those sarcastic but serious things I sometimes say. (General Kelly told me today he didn't want Reince's job, but I'll keep at him. Management 101.) Jeff Sessions had his very smart number-two, Rosenberg, Rothstein, whatever, write up the press release of our "reasons"—which I have to tell you made me laugh, since it was all about how Comey had been so unfair to poor, poor Hillary during the campaign. And *boom*, get him out of here, bye-bye, Comey gone. I felt a little better for a day or so.

★ ★

HALF THE JOB OF BEING PRESIDENT is meeting with foreign officials, right? So, what, I was supposed to cancel my meeting with the Russian secretary of state and the other one, the big fat one, the ambassador, just because it was the day after I fired the nut job Comey for not stopping the fake Russia stories and finding the leakers? Of course not! It would've been very rude and very weak. It was a good thing I didn't cancel, I can tell you that—because that day the Russians and I were figuring out how to combine our intel with their intel and Israel's intel, although I never once mentioned Israel, to stop ISIS from pulling off another 9/11.

★ ★ ★ ★ ★ ★ ★ ★ ★

THE "SPECIAL COUNSEL" IS TOTALLY RIGGED

L ike everyone these days, I get some of my most interesting information from the Internet, although usually it's printed out, because so many extremely important things never make it into the fake media. After I fired Comey, which I decided to do on the seventh day of May, I found an article through the Twitter called "Seven Days in May 2017." *Seven Days in May* is the movie where generals are plotting a coup against the president because he's trying to make peace with Russia. I saw it in high school with my parents at the Utopia Theater in Queens, right after Kennedy was killed, and it had a big impact on me, although I remember my dad shaking his head and muttering at the end because he'd been rooting for Burt Lancaster and the other generals. Anyway, this Internet article says the same thing is actually happening now, with Comey and Clapper and this General Hayden as Burt Lancaster and Kirk Douglas, and Trump as the hero. A lot of people on the Internet, and I mean a lot, so many MAGA people, agreed that it was probably true.

As soon as I read that I felt a strong need to warn people what could be happening, that it was an emergency, but without specifically mentioning *Seven Days in May*, which I knew would make everybody go crazy. Which is why I beamed out six tweets during the next hour of *Fox & Friends*—"collusion between Russia and Trump fabricated by Dems as an excuse for losing," "Fake Media working overtime," "maybe cancel future 'press briefings,'" "Comey better hope there are no 'tapes' of our conversations," "everyone with knowledge of the witch hunt says there is no collusion." Good.

★ ★ ★ ★ ★ ★ ★ ★ ★ ★ ★ ★ ★ ★ ★ ★ ★ ★ ★ ★

SESSIONS'S NUMBER-TWO, the guy who dreamed up the story that I fired Comey because of how he'd treated Hillary, which I do still get a kick out of, turned out to be so sneaky a week later when he hired the "special counsel" to look into "Russia." I'm not going to call him a Judas, because I don't use that kind of language, but many people are saying that. After my one tweet about how they never appointed a "special counsel" to investigate the crimes of the Obama Administration or Hillary's campaign, everybody on my team advised me to stop—except Jared. Jared was pushing me to go on the attack against this guy Mueller, although I knew it was just one of those Jared moments I've seen a lot in the White House, where he's around guys like Steve and Kosher Steve and McGahn and me so he goes out of his way to look tough. On the other hand, they say the FBI and the "special counsel" are now investigating him—that Jared's "a person of interest"—so maybe it's also because he has skin in the game, no atheists in foxholes, cornered rats bite, et cetera.

Not that the "special counsel" isn't totally rigged. And not just because "recused" scaredy-cat Sessions refuses to protect the presidency—Mueller went to prep school with John Kerry *and* he's an old friend of Comey's. These tall, skinny Boy Scout WASP phonies have their own club that's against Trump and regular Americans. My father warned me about it when I was a kid, the same club, when John Lindsay, the mayor of New York, ran it. When I mentioned Lindsay to Bannon he looked it up and found out he actually went to the *same prep school* as Mueller and Kerry and the same college as Kerry, and he was six foot four, another tall WASP phony who wanted the media and the minorities to love him and couldn't care less about real people. It's scary.

★ ★ ★ ★ ★ ★ ★ ★ ★ ★ ★ ★ ★ ★ ★ ★ ★ ★ ★ ★

ALTHOUGH YOU HAVE TO hand it to them—all those guys do look the part. As we were discussing replacements for Comey, I was very strong on needing somebody who looked the part, "a real central casting FBI director"—which led me to what I call one of my eureka moments: Ivanka is now in discussions with the actual company in Hollywood, in Burbank, Central Casting, about expanding into public-sector job recruiting, with the very strong provision that The Trump Organization couldn't acquire the firm until after my presidency.

★ ★ ★ ★ ★ ★ ★ ★ ★ ★ ★ ★ ★ ★ ★ ★ ★ ★ ★ ★

WITH THE FAKE MEDIA GOING CRAZY, totally making up new fake stories, it was great to get away to the Middle East and Europe, where nobody cared about Comey or Russia or all of the other fake news.

They love Trump in Saudi Arabia, which is the headquarters of Islam, which proves I'm not "Islamophobic" whatsoever. The king personally met me at the airport (which he didn't do for Obama and, trust me, wouldn't have done for "President Hillary") and he gave me their national gold medal, which only goes to the very best people, and they projected a beautiful 100-foot-high face of Trump on the Ritz-Carlton, like the Wizard of Oz, and then showed me a special glowing glass ball, also like in *The Wizard of Oz*.

Although I was very, very disappointed to have to miss the KitchenAid Senior PGA Championship at my Trump National Golf Club outside Washington over Memorial Day weekend. I wasn't surprised the tournament didn't air in Saudi Arabia, but why not Italy or Belgium? I brought it up at our G7 summit, along with the shocking lockout of Fox News from so many of the foreign TV systems, during my discussions of unfair European trade policies.

★ ★

DURING THE TRIP I went ten days without hitting a golf ball. Ten days without sleeping or eating at a Trump property. And ten days without beaming a single true, great, personal Trump tweet that tells the truth that the people love. So I proved I can do it. It's very hard, but I can do it. I have great willpower, some of the greatest willpower. But coming home from Europe and the Middle East and Israel, being able to tweet and golf freely, and eat what I want, I realized all over again why we love America.

★ ★ ★ ★ ★ ★ ★ ★ ★

EVERYONE NERVOUS EXCEPT ME

Did you notice the radical Islamic terrorists only killed people in England and Iran right *after* Trump left Europe and the Middle East? That wasn't a coincidence. I keep everything around me safe. Another Trump "superpower." The fake media didn't write about that.

And my tweets after the London attacks about their weak Islamic mayor and about my Muslim ban that my politically correct "Justice" Department wouldn't do, *those* tweets were so great, so true, so honest, so important, so fantastic, so tough, from the heart, some of my best, no lawyers, no puppet. *Everyone* listening. *Everyone* nervous. Except me! And because of the radical Islamic terrorism, which I still say—*radical Islamic terrorism, radical Islamic terrorism, radical Islamic terrorism*—for days nobody paid attention to any of the fake Russia stories.

★ ★ ★ ★ ★ ★ ★ ★ ★ ★ ★ ★ ★ ★ ★ ★ ★ ★ ★ ★

IN FACT, OVER THE SUMMER, as you know, the Russia business finally started to fade away. Which is why I didn't accept Jeff Sessions's nervous little offer to resign the first time he did it. Even though I think he did it and leaked it because he thought it'd make it harder for me to fire him later. By the way, it would've been nice if Jared had offered to resign, too. It would be nice if everyone offered to resign. Not that I'd accept them all, but it would show respect. And the ones I kept would be so grateful, they'd love their president even more. Management 101. But now I've got my own lawyers on the Russia hoax and the "obstruction of justice" case, guys I pay, led by this guy Kasowitz, worked for me on my casinos, on my divorces, on my libel suits, on my university, fantastic Roy Cohn type, scary-tough, and he's put together a whole team, other scary-tough Jewish lawyers with glasses and good hair. So tough, so scary, the scariest and toughest, who hate the WASP phonies like Mueller as much as I do.

Anyhow, as you're reading this many months or many years later, it's very possible you don't even remember any of the fake "Russia" stories. Because they were fake. As Rodrigo said to me this morning, *"Ang kita sa bula something something something,"* which means "What comes from bubbles will disappear in bubbles." I think Rodrigo is the wisest man I have ever known, in a different way than Roy Cohn was wise.

> **AS YOU'RE READING THIS MANY MONTHS OR MANY YEARS LATER, IT'S VERY POSSIBLE YOU DON'T EVEN REMEMBER ANY OF THE FAKE "RUSSIA" STORIES. BECAUSE THEY WERE FAKE.**

★ ★

I LET COMEY TESTIFY TO CONGRESS, to have his last bit of time in the spotlight, such a showboat, and leak our confidential conversations to the public, because I'm not worried. Except for his total lies about me, especially when he called me a liar, he totally vindicated me. By the way, one of the reasons I wanted to get rid of Comey is because I know he would've made a big stink about one of my secret projects. Which Jeff Sessions went ahead and arranged "on the down-low," as Ivanka said when I visited New York City in June—in the federal prison in Brooklyn, I met for an hour with El Chapo, the Mexican drug lord, who's a bad guy, yes, but also a very smart cookie, very tough, and very, very successful. They're going to hate that I'm telling you about it here, but I think it's important for Americans to know— one, how hard I work and so much of it is invisible to you; two, it proves I care about the issues of "incarceration"; and three, it proves I get along great with the Mexicans. Actually, El Chapo and I found out we had a lot of common ground— on the importance of loyalty and never giving up, and how much we both enjoy the love of the regular people.

★ ★

THE FIRST LADY MOVED into the White House at the end of the school year. Everyone was saying how nice it is that we can finally be together. So true.

But having Barron around really is totally fantastic! He's like an adult now, very much on my wavelength. I convinced his mother he needed to move to the White House permanently, go to a top school around here, become one of his dad's advisers, maybe get school credit for that.

The First Lady agreed after spending a major amount of time discussing it, *very* major when "time" costs the $1,200 an hour you're paying lawyers to help figure it out. The First Lady will be living full-time in the White House, too, through January 21, 2021, depending on contingencies, et cetera, which is great.

★ ★ ★ ★ ★ ★ ★ ★ ★ ★ ★ ★ ★ ★ ★ ★ ★ ★ ★

I REALIZE NOW in a way I never did before I was president how much fake news there really is—and I don't just mean Russia and negative polls. But the untrue stories about how our fantastic health plan and tax cuts will help rich people more than everyone else. Fake news. Or how the race car driver Ryan Newman, who loves Trump, didn't win the Indy 500 this year—that he was beaten by some *Japanese* guy. Fake news. Just like right around the same time, in Belgium, after I told the NATO leaders to stop being free-loaders, the fake media just kept showing the clip of me saying hi to the head of Montenegro at our photo op, like I was being rude. Fake news. And like in Sicily, when Anthony and the rest of the Secret Service guys insisted, for security reasons, that I ride in a secure golf cart through the town instead of walking the half mile along with the other leaders (who nobody really wants to assassi-nate), the biased fake media used that to make me look bad, too. Fake news.

By the way, Montenegro wasn't even officially a member of NATO then. Also, you probably didn't realize that the Clintons broke Yugoslavia into like ten different countries, and three of them are now in NATO, which is so unfair, like if Vermont and Massachusetts and Connecticut were all allowed to join the UN. Also, speaking of Montenegro, it's really barely even a country, less population than North Dakota, and the people are considered poor and lazy by people in the other, better former Yugoslavias, such as Slovenia. The biased American media never writes that.

Even the social media is biased, even though they don't have "editors," and even though Trump has *made* their businesses and they should be paying me royalties. No surprise, Twitter is head-quartered in San Francisco, which voted 91 percent for Hillary, so they won't admit that Trump has *135* million followers, not *35* mil-lion, more than Katy Perry or Barack Obama or anybody else. By the way, why do Khloé and Kourtney Kardashian *and* Kendall and Kylie Jenner all have almost exactly the same number of Twitter followers? Something's going on, and we're going to appoint a special social media commission, the first ever, to find out.

And speaking of fake media out to get Trump, I just found out they're all set to prevent *You Can't Spell America Without Me* from winning the Pulitzer Prize next spring. This book *should* be the first autobiography to win the Pulitzer since they gave it twenty years ago to Katharine Graham of the *Washington Post*, and *should* be the first book by a president to win in *sixty* years, since John F. Kennedy, whose book was actually written by a ghostwriter, unlike this one. But it turns out the Pulitzer Prizes are rigged, given out *to* the dishonest media *by* the dishonest media, not by the actual Pulitzer family I used to know in Palm Beach who make the nice Florida dresses. It's all rigged against us. It's all fake.

★ ★ ★ ★ ★ ★ ★ ★ ★

IS JARED A FREDO?

S omeone who's no longer so young herself asked me today at Camp David in her "cute" accent if turning seventy-one on Wednesday is what made me "right away do these two mornings of the tweets that only make every-thing bad and worse." And the answer is *no*, the president has *no choice* but to keep communicating the *truth*.

Because, like I said, the fake news media really does *hate* when I go around them and use my very powerful social media to tell more than one hundred million people, Trump's troops, that this *is* the greatest witch hunt in American history and the Judas who told me to fire the FBI director *is* investigating me for firing the FBI director, and his pathetic little mouse of a boss won't stop him. And people don't even know that crooked Hillary and her family and staff have all kinds of dealings with Russia and that she destroyed her cell phones with a hammer like a crazy person and obstructed justice with Obama's attorney general.

That's what I tweeted the last couple of days. And *no*, I do *not* need to change my supplements and vitamins.

Camp David? Even worse than I imagined. The one Saturday night was plenty. It's the kind of place your friends' parents had in the Poconos, the kind of place you get rich or become president to *avoid* spending weekends. *One* pathetic golf hole, not even full size, a hundred yards and a green, hole in one, hole in one, hole in one, no fucking fun at all, pardon my French. They do have a Camp David gift shop, good for them, it's called the Shangri-la, but virtually no Trump merchandise.

> *MITZI: Presidential to-do list*
> *Song, "HOLE IN ONE, HOLE IN ONE, HOLE IN ONE /*
> *NO F-STAR-STAR-STAR-STAR-STAR-STAR FUN /*
> *SHANGRI-LA," © 2017 by Donald J. Trump.*

★ ★ ★ ★ ★ ★ ★ ★ ★ ★ ★ ★ ★ ★ ★ ★ ★ ★ ★

I ALWAYS KNEW PEOPLE LIKE SPICER AND REINCE wouldn't be permanent. I knew it for sure with Reince a month before my landslide victory, after the fake media released the unauthorized *Access Hollywood* tape, and Reince said I should drop out of the race. Weak. At our first full cabinet meeting in June, where we went around the table and each of them explained how I was making them make America great again, and Reincey said, "We thank you for the opportunity and the blessing to serve your agenda," it was actually pathetic, *so* desperate to keep his job. Literally on the way out of that meeting I asked Kelly again if he'd take over. Although to be fair, Reince was useful because from his reactions to things I always knew how the hypocrites and weaklings in Washington were going to react to the things Trump does.

Unlike Jared. Jared pushed me to trust Mike Flynn. He was sure the Democrats would be happy to see Comey fired. He thought it was okay to raise money in China for *his* family's real estate business by using the President Trump brand. He tried to get *my* White House counsel to give him a public Good Housekeeping seal of approval on the Russia thing. He wouldn't stop trying to get me to surrender to our enemies on the horrible Paris climate deal and to get rid of Bannon—especially now that Steve had his people push out the news about Jared's Soros deal, which I didn't know was going to happen in advance, as I told Ivanka, because if I had known I wouldn't have smiled when I saw it in *Breitbart*. "Jared," I finally told him, "only Ivanka can fire you, and I'm not firing Steve." Although I might, but not because Jared hates him.

Jared reminds me of President Macaroon, and I'll bet thirty years from now Ivanka will be as great-looking as Mrs. Macaroon, who I had great, great chemistry with in Paris—I mean, *whoa*, sixty-four, truly unbelievable, almost as old as my first wife. Except unlike Macaroon, Jared wouldn't have pulled the stunt with the handshake. Jared doesn't have much of a handshake. In fact, is Jared a Fredo? I'm starting to worry he's a Fredo who thinks he's a Michael.

★ ★ ★ ★ ★ ★ ★ ★ ★

WE'RE BOTH STRONG AND KNOW THE SCORE

═══════════════════════════════════
═══════════════════════════════════

Since everybody except the fake media and the Democrats and paid protesters and Hillary finally realized that the Russia stories were a complete and total ruse and hoax—a hoax set up starting like three hundred years ago, I've recently heard, by what they call the Illuminati, so scary, so bad—I was finally "allowed" to meet with Putin, at the big European leaders meeting in Germany right after the Fourth of July. I knew from my special NSC chart that Putin isn't a big guy, but for such a strong, strong, strong leader he is so *unbelievably* short, much shorter than my junior special presidential assistant, Barron, if you can believe it. At one of the photo sessions I tried to make Merkel and Putin stand back-to-back to prove she's taller.

At my official meeting with Putin, I didn't want my national security adviser there, General McMaster, because the whole military thing would've given it a harsh vibe. "So I need to get this out of the way, Vladimir, okay?" I said. "Did you do it—'interfere' with our election?" He said very vehemently, "No, I did not, absolutely not." Then I asked him a second time, but in a totally different way—I stared into his eyes, deep, the way my mother taught me. She always said, "You stare into someone's eyes, you don't flinch at all, and they can't help but tell you the truth." Like when she'd go, "Don, did you take the ten dollars from my purse?" with the stare, I was done. Usually. So in Hamburg I did the staring thing with Putin the second time I asked—"You really weren't involved in our election at all?"—and he said again, "Absolutely not." And I said, "Okay, good, but you know, we can't have any doubt about our elections, especially since the fake news in America is still exaggerating about it, and I'll probably have to sign this sanctions bill, but okay, whatever, let's you and I move forward. In fact, let's figure out how we can do cybersecurity together. And destroy ISIS, and solve Syria. Okay?" He did ask me how Israel got that ISIS intel I told his foreign minister about in May, but I just smiled and made the zipped-lips motion, which is the same in Russian.

We also discussed history, how Germany had tried to destroy America and freedom, and he talked about how Russia and America had won World War II against the Germans together, which many people don't realize, and wondered how Americans would feel if the Mexicans took back Texas and California, because those itsy-bitsy "NATO" countries up north all used to be part of Russia. We also had a chance to figure out why the two of us have such a strong natural bond, almost like brothers, aside from how we're both strong and know the score. The toughest moments in both of our lives, the ones that didn't kill us but made us stronger, happened *right at the same time*—the Soviet Union fell apart *exactly* when some of my companies were declaring "bankruptcy," and people thought Trump and Putin were finished. And then the New York banks squeezed Russia just like they squeezed me, but we both came back, stronger and better and richer than ever, superpowers again.

We chatted some more at dinner that night for a few minutes or an hour or whatever, which the sick fake media pretended was bad. I can now reveal why I went over to talk with him. Putin was seated next to the First Lady, *my* First Lady, who actually used to be one of his citizens when it was all communist over there, he probably speaks some Slovenian, so when I looked over and saw them talking so closely, the First Lady laughing and enjoying herself like she almost never does, I realized I had a duty to go over and make sure nothing negative for America happened. But later in Hamburg, he and I had a final private moment together, and this was secret until now, just the two of us walking through the mist by the North Sea at night. I said, "Vladimir, I think this is the beginning of a beautiful friendship," but my Bogart impression wasn't perfect, so he maybe didn't completely get it.

★ ★

THE FAKE MEDIA has been talking for days about a nothing meeting Don Junior had with some Russian lady more than a year ago, before Russia fever existed, before I was even nominated for president, and since this is a book about my presidency, quite frankly it's inappropriate to be talking about it here. Although for the record, even though he's also "Donald Trump," the real Donald Trump did not know about that meeting, wouldn't have gone to that meeting, and if I had, wouldn't have switched my story about it twice in three days and put out my own e-mails that made me look bad—if I even used e-mails, which I don't, and this proves once and for all I've always been very, very right about that.

Speaking of cyber, that Silicon Valley ninja who broke into the White House on Barron's birthday just pleaded guilty *on the same day* that Hawaiian judge with the white last name, Watson, which is the same as the biggest supercomputer, ruled against us again on the travel ban. And the Chinese all of a sudden decide to build their computer factory in Wisconsin. And Xi is calling me all the time telling me to calm down about North Korea. Something really is going on with the Orientals.

★ ★

FINALLY GOT THE MOOCH HIRED! He'll fix our communications—so, Management 101 *and* Marketing 101. "The president has really good karma," he announced on his first day, and "he's genuinely a wonderful human being." Gotta love the Mooch!

★ ★

THE MOOCH DIDN'T WORK OUT, and because he never officially worked in the White House—that's 100 percent true, you can look it up—he wasn't actually fired, so no harm no foul. Plus, I made him famous, just like I made Reince and Spicer and Omarosa famous, all so famous. I think they're grateful. They should be.

★ ★

CAN YOU BELIEVE that nobody wrote about how great we've done at the end of the first *two hundred* days? All the important legislation we passed, the most ever, not counting repeal and replace, which the Republicans couldn't get done, they let a guy with a terrible brain problem vote it down, McCain, Jesus, loser, disgraceful. And don't forget all the jobs we created, the most ever, keeping the illegals out, the highest stock market ever, no war, so amazing, so successful. Not a word. Fake media.

★ ★ ★ ★ ★ ★ ★ ★ ★

IF ANYTHING HAPPENS TO ME, HERE'S THE TRUTH

I have to admit I enjoyed telling Jared he was reporting to General Kelly from now on. I was even okay with Kelly announcing on his first day as chief of staff that the president has 100 percent confidence in Jeff Sessions and General McMaster, because what does that even really mean? It's not like a contract. I can fire them both right this second if that 100 percent confidence all of a sudden drops to zero percent.

But I'm actually sick of my generals, of all people, trying to make me look weaker, Mattis and McMaster and now Kelly, and also Tillerson, who was like a five-star business general. They say I can't rip up the terrible Iran nuclear deal, I have to sign the terrible Russian sanctions bill that ties my hands on making a great deal, I have to slow down on getting the transvestites out of the Army—making it like I need to ask their permission to do anything. Even tweet! Trump doesn't ask permission, and President Trump especially does not do *May I, pretty please*.

The fake media is saying now that General Kelly was so upset when I fired the crazy crooked leaker Comey that he talked about resigning.

No *May I* for Trump, no Trump *May I*—which reminds me: the *Seven Days in May* thing may be real, someone I trust on these things tells me, even though now it's August. But maybe it's planned for *next* May? Maybe that's why they're making me send more soldiers to Afghanistan?

If anything happens to me, here's the truth, on the record, part of history.

★ ★ ★ ★ ★ ★ ★ ★ ★

WE'LL ALL LOOK BACK AND LAUGH ABOUT THIS

W hile I'm here in New Jersey at the Northwestern White House, owned by Trump, which many top experts in addition to Anthony tell me has the most defensible terrain and best weapons-system positions of any Trump property, at the old White House in Washington they're replacing the air-conditioning system. While they're at it I'm also having them install new carpeting, *truly great* carpeting, and paint the walls—Obama had all *yellow* carpets and *yellow* walls, which I frankly find disgusting. Reminds me of that Men's Wearhouse, Sy Syms tan suit he wore.

The White House air conditioning they're replacing was installed during George Bush's first administration, back when he didn't have the southern accent at all, when he was fresh out of the CIA, which makes me think it may not just be "air conditioning," if you know what I mean. I think you know what I mean. Barron says I should learn sign language from Internet videos, and make the people in the White House I trust learn it, Ivanka and whoever, so the bugging can't work. Such a brilliant kid.

The fake media is so upset about what I said on Venezuela about military options—but what they don't know is that I had an understanding with Nick Maduro down there, concerning trade, future hospitality development, so when he welshed I had no choice but to hit back. And the fake media is even more upset about my latest tweets against North Korea. *Trust me*, okay, the North Korea thing will work out fine, *so* fine, not to worry, you can't imagine, we've got it covered, I can't tell you the amazing top-top-top-secret way we've got North Korea covered, but we do. After we win there, and after everybody knows we've won, talk about a "twist ending," we'll all look back and laugh about it. I can't wait.

For the record, what Bannon said about North Korea wasn't why I let General Kelly can him, and it wasn't because Jared is scared of him, either. I still think Steve is my Tom Hagen, and originally *Godfather III* was supposed to be all about Michael Corleone and Tom becoming enemies—spooky, right? Speaking of spooky, I'm hungry all the time and have to pee constantly, which might mean I have diabetes, which would be another thing I have in common with Michael.

★ ★ ★ ★ ★ ★ ★ ★ ★

CALL HIM FLIPPER

Since I became president, I've sometimes hummed "Hail to the Chief" in bed at night, to relax and fall asleep. But now if I *don't* do it I can't sleep at all, but as soon as I start, the theme song to *Flipper* starts running through my head, competing with it, and with a laugh track of mean laughter, like the devil in this cartoon I saw that scared me so much when I was little. I hum "Hail to the Chief" louder but the *Flipper* song gets louder, too, and every time in the song they sing "They call him Flipper, Flipper!" I see Jared's face or Paul Manafort's or Mike Flynn's. I don't see Steve Bannon's face, but I'm not sure if that means I can trust him more. It's like a nightmare, but worse, because I can't wake up, because I'm already awake.

★ ★ ★ ★ ★ ★ ★ ★ ★

IT'S A CRAZY WORLD

They say it's almost fall, and the calendar on my phone says September, but to be perfectly honest I have a very strong belief it's still summer, I have a hunch somebody screwed up with daylight saving time, made it happen too early and is now covering it up; Wilbur Ross in the Commerce Department is looking into that. Because I think it was just this week that Ivanka was crying, telling me I couldn't say what I wanted to say at the big African American convention, the N-word double-A battery double-dip double-stuffed for colored people, on the double—their convention is in the summer in Baltimore, I know that, that's how I memorized it, because the blacks love the summer. My speech was about jobs, all the jobs I'm going to create, so many fantastic jobs, unemployment so low we'll need to put children and elderly people to work, unemployment down to zero, I wanted to say to the blacks, "Work will set you free! Work will set you free!"—make it a new Trump chant, like "Lock her up! Lock her up!" but *positive*, like "America First," and I said to my team when they got so upset, "Hey, I'm a very strong believer in hard work, I don't *know* German, I don't know 'Free Fatty Arbuckle' or whatever you say it is in German," I never knew German, only my dad's "*Sieg ist mein*" and a few others, but very, very few of the African Americans would know the concentration camp slogan anyway, I'm sure, because I didn't.

Although if Ivanka hadn't stopped me from giving that speech, then afterward, during those fights between the protesters in Charlottesville, both sides, definitely both sides, the fake media would have brought that up to say that Trump is a "Nazi." So Ivanka does have the Trump seeing-the-future superpower. She's got the super genes.

By the way, the leader in Charlottesville who likes Trump so much, Duke, the *Duke of Hazzard* with the plastic surgery, I have never met or spoken to him in my life. I don't think my father knew him either.

Speaking of Charlottesville and my father, he always said you have to realize the blacks are pissed off, permanently pissed off, even when they're acting nice, which is also why he sometimes told me I was "acting like a spoiled little N-word," except back then you could say the real word even if you weren't black. He said what people didn't realize is the welfare and the free apartments and all the rest made them even angrier, which is why they started rioting in the sixties, because although the handouts make liberals feel better, like they're making up for slavery, the handouts are actually just continuing slavery, *and* it costs more—so lose-lose.

I took a lifeguard test in Queens one summer. Phil Adamo was the head lifeguard, and Phil told me how sometimes you need to smack the drowning man or he'll bring you both down. So sometimes people in trouble, not just black people, I'm not racist, I'm the least racist person, they need a good smack to bring them back to self-respect. That's Management 101, 102, 103, 104.

Anthony wasn't on duty during the Charlottesville weekend. Why?

I didn't need *Merkel* telling me the "Nazis" in Charlottesville were "repulsive" and "evil," or the CEOs, so ungrateful, and then my own top generals, the real ones, who run the Army and Navy, all five of them grandstanding about "Nazis" and "racists" to make me look bad—and doing it on social media, copying Trump! So weak.

Something is definitely going on.

★ ★

BEST THING ABOUT THE SUMMER was no *SNL*, which is a show that I made successful after it was completely failing, and should have been canceled twenty-five years ago, but wasn't, because Lorne Michaels, who's a Canadian immigrant, maybe legal, maybe not, so ungrateful, must have terrible dirt on the executives at RCA *and* General Electric *and* Comcast. And I have a great sense of humor, but the hater Alec "Phone Message" Baldwin is so bad at playing me, like he's doing Aldo Ray or somebody. He and his brothers were like the

BEST THING ABOUT THE SUMMER WAS NO *SNL.*

Bowery Boys of Long Island, famous losers, all big mouths and no balls, although the young one, Stephen, is good people. Before he went "born again," I'm told he was like the David Bowie of Massapequa, grade A pervert, although that's true of many of the born-agains before they become "born again."

But my point is, the entire media, entertainment, the movies, even some of the telephone systems, the news, all of them always take such a terrible tone concerning President Trump, like all of them are pretending to be my father—almost all of them—saying I'm no good even though I'm actually *not* a bad person, so the hatred, such hatred, so much hatred, I hate the hatred, the constant hits, the anti-Trump, the viciousness and venom are like a disgusting epidemic. And the betrayal. So much betrayal of Trump, so many terrible people. As the Filipino people say in Tag-along, "*Mahirap mamatay ang masamang damo*," meaning, "The weeds are difficult to kill." But eventually you do kill them, and then it's beautiful and perfect, like all my golf courses, not a single weed on the greens or even the fairways.

I said I wouldn't brag anymore. But no golfer until now, ever in the history of this country, has ever shot eighteen straight holes in one. So unfair and sad we haven't been able to talk about it. And I don't just mean "sad" in the Twitter way. After Ivanka said I had to keep that score secret until I was out of office, when we release the taxes, I actually sobbed, first time since before I was a grown-up.

Why don't they ever say, "Wow, he's totally prevented nuclear, almost a year as president and no nuclear at all!" I talk the nuclear card, maybe that's what got us victory, all options, all options on the table, you always have to have all options, but in the meantime I haven't used it, haven't played the card. Will I ever go to war? I hope not, maybe not, I don't think so, probably not, could happen, not soon, but look, I don't want to answer, I can't answer, because national security but also *they* shouldn't know, the war enemies, ISIS, Venezuela, Korea, Hawaii, so I don't want to say I won't or I will, which has been one of the problems with our country— I don't want anyone to know what Trump is thinking, which they have ways of doing, very scary, actually they *think* they have ways of doing but we now have major, major scientific ways of preventing it in all of the White Houses, I can tell you that—from what I understand, my brilliant uncle at MIT, the great engineer John Trump, was one of the inventors of that. So we'll give him a medal in 2018.

It's a crazy world out there, so crazy, crazier all the time, I've never seen anything like it, the amount of press that I'm getting is just crazy, absolutely crazy, because I do know my subject, I'm prepared to take the test, you know, the pop quiz but also the final exam, and I do know our country couldn't continue to do what it was doing. They didn't respect us and they were laughing at us, laughing, laughing, laughing, that I can tell you.

★ ★ ★ ★ ★ ★ ★ ★ ★

SO MANY, MANY SECRETS TO KEEP

D r. Müller and I had a nice talk. She brought me some new supplements. She said they'll last through October. They're very good. I'm very good. I'm very relaxed. I'm great.

The last chapter was very, very visionary. I let Barron read it. He says it needs fixing. He says there's an editor "app" that can do it for me.

I'm almost finished. With the book, not the presidency, ha ha ha, no way. Being president is demanding. Dr. Müller and Ivanka say that between the tweeting and the book, I'm spending too much time away from "being president." Okay.

I asked the Pentagon to invent an app where I say a sentence and then the app takes my thoughts from that one sentence and expands them into a few pages. They say it might take a while. So I'm going to be more brief from now on, but you can expand these shorter chapters later if you want, when the app comes out.

The other reason I'm going to be more brief is because of national security. It's become even more important, very, very important, *shhhh*, so many, many secrets to keep.

Like the big one about North Korea. I won't give it away. But I will say this: Paul McCartney has been a fake since the real Paul died, because the Beatles were worth like $100 billion a year to the economy of England, so British intelligence, the same ones who wiretapped me for Obama, gave some auto mechanic a lot of plastic surgery and turned him into "Sir Paul."

The secrets and dangers are also why I need to stay inside more. But I can tell you we are planning so many great secret things as we finish the first year, such fantastic things. You'll be surprised. *America First—And America Last*. Like it? Me, too.

★ ★ ★ ★ ★ ★ ★ ★ ★

ROUTE 66

hen I sell this book I can charge the publisher *by the chapter*. I could get to sixty-six chapters.

Mike Pence told me there are sixty-six books in the Bible, and I told him the address of Jared's building on Fifth Avenue, which is half as tall as Trump Tower, is 666, which made Mike mutter some special Christian words. Christ died at thirty-three, which is half of sixty-six, and my father's middle name was Christ.

At Trump Tower, the Northern White House starts on the sixty-sixth floor.

I have sixty-six years of memories, starting in 1951, right after Dad got "rich" and we moved into the new house on Midland Parkway, which looks like the White House. It cost $66,000.

I got to second base with Mitzi when I was fourteen, watching the show *Route 66* on TV. She said I looked like Tod, the one played by Martin Milner, who was later on *Adam-12* around 1966.

Today I asked why we haven't won in Afghanistan yet and some-one said it hasn't been very long, so then I asked how long ago I announced the new plan, and he said, "Sixty-six days, Mr. President. Only sixty-six."

"Hannity and chill," as Ivanka says: Working hard late into the night at the White House, I take little breaks, like Edison and Einstein did—but unlike them, I boost my energy with a phenomenal slice of chocolate cake from the nearby Trump International Hotel.

★ ★ ★ ★ ★ ★ ★ ★

MAGA

Lots of my MAGA people on the Internet are saying extraterrestrials have infiltrated the government, especially "intelligence." I have many reasons to believe it's true. This time I'm not going to make the mistake I did with the "wiretap" on me in Trump Tower, when I "let my anger get the best of me," as Ivanka says, and I wasn't taking the right supplements, so now I'm having my people gather the proof first before I start tweeting about it. It will be incredible when the truth comes out. I can't get more specific yet, but you know how Trump was the one who was saying Obama wasn't born in America? Maybe he was born a billion miles from here.

★ ★ ★ ★ ★ ★ ★ ★ ★

MY NOBEL PRIZE

I've heard people around the White House a few times lately whispering about "the twenty-fifth" and "plans for the twenty-fifth," "is Pence on board for the twenty-fifth," and so on. It turns out it's a surprise twenty-fifth birthday party for my daughter Tiffany, who's apparently here in Washington at Georgetown Law School now, later in October. Nice.

★ ★ ★ ★ ★ ★ ★ ★ ★ ★ ★ ★ ★ ★ ★ ★ ★ ★ ★

I GOT A CALL from someone in Sweden who spoke English with a Swedish accent. She said I shouldn't be disappointed on Monday when the Nobel Peace Prize is announced. I don't get it, because they've already decided to give me my Nobel Prize *next* October, in 2018, unless I start a *really* big war between now and then ha ha ha. "Done," I said. Nice. Also, it'll be just before the midterm elections. Fantastic.

★ ★ ★ ★ ★ ★ ★ ★ ★

SHLIMAZEL

After dinner at Ivanka and Jared's on Saturday night, after their very special Shlimazel Day of Atonement ended, I said I wanted to go for a walk with them and the kids along Rock Creek to look at the Halloween decorations.

"Oh, look," I said after we'd walked two blocks, "there's the Obamas' house! Let's knock on the door and say hello!" But Ivanka's a smart girl. She knew I just wanted to make him admit he wiretapped me, and all the rest, so she and Anthony wouldn't let me go. "We don't want another incident like last Tuesday, Dad."

She was talking about how I walked downstairs into the public area of the White House one morning in my pajamas and handed out autographed 2016 voting maps to a few of the visitors on tour, the map that shows my incredible landslide in electoral votes, which by the way the tourists loved and then agreed not to talk about after the new head usher, Dr. Müller's friend, gave them all their special cash prizes.

★ ★ ★ ★ ★ ★ ★ ★

ANG BUHLAY AY MAGANDA

I'm pretty sure they're taking my phone away when I'm sleeping to check my drafts on Twitter, the amazing ones I haven't beamed out yet. So I asked Rodrigo to get me extra phones, secret phones, what they call the "burners." He needs to buy them with cash, so we came up with a great way to do that—every night I sign the tie I wore that day with a Sharpie, which he then sells in a special market on the Internet.

★ ★ ★ ★ ★ ★ ★ ★ ★ ★ ★ ★ ★ ★ ★ ★ ★ ★

"ANTHONY," I asked, "is it true your Secret Service lie detectors are the gold standard, the best there are?"

"I believe that's correct, Mr. President."

"Okay, great. This weekend the First Lady and I are going to play 'Truth or Dare,' and to make it more fun, more presidential, I want to hook her up to one of your lie detectors, with one of your expert guys running it. Okay?"

"That would be a serious breach of regulations, Mr. President."

Rodrigo *did* bring up the possibility that my first and third wives might *both* be Russian agents, working for Putin, since they both grew up in the Communist countries back then and the First Lady's dad, Viktor, was an actual Communist official. I really, really hope it isn't true. But it might be. Keith, my security guy, *my* security guy in all the White Houses, worked for me for twenty years, is going to check it out.

My wife is almost forty-eight. I've literally never been with a woman that old. I stopped things with Ivana when she was forty, when we'd been together thirteen years; I stopped things with Marla when she was thirty-five. My wife and I have been married for almost thirteen years. When Rodrigo said to me *"Ang buhlay ay maganda,"* I was shocked, because I thought he was being funny, saying, "Angry that Melania's getting laid" or something, because Rodrigo really never jokes around. But it was just another Tag-along proverb—it means "Get it while you can."

★ ★ ★ ★ ★ ★ ★ ★ ★ ★ ★ ★ ★ ★ ★ ★ ★ ★ ★

HOPE HICKS, my very loyal and very beautiful director of strategic communications, Hopester, just turned twenty-nine. I just reread the statement she issued about me at the beginning of the summer completely on her own. One of Rodrigo's relatives printed it up in that fancy art writing they use on wedding invitations, so I can refer to it whenever I want. "President Trump," it says, "has a magnetic personality and exudes positive energy, which is infectious to those around him. He is brilliant with a great sense of humor and an amazing ability to make people feel special and aspire to be more than even they thought possible."

Beautiful, right?

I think we'll put it on our White House Christmas card this year.

★ ★

HOPE AND CHANGE. That's going to be a new Trump slogan. I thought of it.

★ ★

OR A VAMPIRE. She used to talk so much about vampires. Or a robot. It could be possible the First Lady is a robot. I actually saw that on the Internet.

> *MITZI:*
> *Is Melania like you? and if so, is it like in*
> The Stepford Wives, *where she's good, or like the*
> *girl in* Blade Runner?

★ ★

I DON'T THINK SO. This morning she stepped on a piece of broken glass that was somehow on the floor right next to her bed and she bled a lot. Plus, Barron definitely came out of her.

★ ★ ★ ★ ★ ★ ★ ★ ★

WAS THAT ALL A DREAM?

D id I just visit London? It's the fall, and I was supposed to. Did I ride in the horse-drawn gold carriage to Buckingham Palace and give the finger to the protesters? During dinner with the queen and all of them did I ask the cute sister of the superhot future queen why she had the same first name as the English race car driver, also cute, blonde, Pippa, and did the royal Pippa tell me she wanted to leave her new husband and become my new First Lady, and did I make out with her a little before Anthony came in and the dinner suddenly stopped and we went away? Or was that a dream?

★ ★ ★ ★ ★ ★ ★ ★ ★

ALL FAKE

I t was all lies, I just found out. I learned the truth. It was all fake.

Mad Dog or Mad Dog's replacement or one of them told me it's *not true* that the reason I shouldn't ever start a war with North Korea is because the CIA had replaced Kim Jong-un with a fake one who secretly works for us. It's still Kim Jong-un.

Rodrigo told me Dr. Müller isn't really a leadership adviser and historian—she's a psychiatrist. Those quizzes she had me take were *psychiatric* tests.

Tiffany turned *twenty-four* in October, not twenty-five. The talk I heard around the White House was about the Twenty-Fifth *Amendment* in the Constitution, where it becomes exactly like *Seven Days in May* and they get rid of me and Mike Pence becomes president.

★ ★ ★ ★ ★ ★ ★ ★ ★ ★

HOORAY PRESIDENT TRUMP, HOORAY PRESIDENTE TRUMP, HOORAY PRESIDENT TRUMP IN RUSSIAN WITH THE CRAZY BACKWARD 3

M y Tag-along proverb Rodrigo sent in with breakfast this morning was the best one yet. *"Kung ano ang kailanman ay hindi mawasak mo bumili ka ng isa pang araw upang sirain ang iba." That which does not destroy you buys you another day to destroy others.*

By the way, remember last year when I was winning in Ohio or Indiana or Iowa, one of those, and I said I could shoot somebody in the middle of Fifth Avenue and I wouldn't lose voters? Well, now I can tell you that wasn't just a "figment of speech." I once *did* shoot someone in the middle of Fifth Avenue—Fifth Avenue in Queens, College Point, near the water, 1966, summer, very late one night, like 3 a.m. in the morning, an argument with this guy who used to work for my dad, betrayed us very badly, we thought he was about to shoot me, and he didn't die, I'm pretty positive. The statute of limitations means they can't prosecute me, and even if they could they can't prove it without me testifying against myself, which isn't allowed because of the Fifth Amendment.

Whoa. Fifth *Amendment*. Fifth *Avenue*.

Right *now* I'm on Fifth Avenue in Manhattan. On the sixty-sixth floor of Trump Tower. The Northern White House.

Inside my special superprivate bedroom in my actual personal private penthouse, PPP, in my true Trump home, the one home totally built *by* Trump, the one *named* Trump, totally *owned* by Trump—as my junior special presidential assistant says, my "Fortress of Solitude."

> MITZI: Presidential to-do list
> Song, "TRUE TRUMP / TOTALLY TOTALLY
> TOTALLY," et cetera, invented and patented by
> President Trump 2017. You definitely got that, Mitzi?
> Okay, thank you. Mitzi, you're so professional and so
> loyal. I totally trust you again.

Finally, I'm here in Trump Tower inside my own special fort, which I just built myself, like the ones I used to build in my bedroom on Midland Parkway, for me alone, but better now, with official *presidential* blankets draped over the chairs, and *gold* chairs, and like a week's supply of Lays and Coke and all my special supplements and vitamins stored right here inside the fort, and my dad can't rip it all apart when he comes home. And now my special secret superagent Anthony just outside the door isn't some *imaginary* genie but a totally *real* genie with real guns who just arrived for his shift and has to die for me if necessary, which is so fantastic. One wall of this fort is glass, Trump Tower glass, dark so nobody can see in, the best glass, bulletproof glass, my window overlooking Fifth Avenue, so I'm looking down at all the beautiful Christmas lights now that it's dark, because President Trump *ended* the War on Christmas, that's what Hannity says and what everyone is saying.

Christmas! New Year's! We're almost at the end of my first three hundred days! Which the fake media won't mention. I need to start planning 2018. Because as I always say, "If you want it done right you have to do it yourself." Which I hear all the time now, but I was actually the first one to ever say it, just like "prime the pump for the economy," which by the way I've done better than any president ever.

> *MITZI: Presidential planning 2018*
>
> *NUMBER ONE: If I didn't already get rid of Mueller, he might die accidentally, or at least get very sick, he's older than me and so many Trump supporters are praying very hard against him.*
>
> *NUMBER TWO: Comey will be locked up for perjury and leaking—Lock him up! Lock him up!— along with Hillary. I could pardon them, I'll tweet about the possibility, but I won't ever do it, and Hillary may die in prison.*

*NUMBER THREE: I will pardon Mike Flynn and
Mike Pence, all of the Mikes, and all of the Steves,
everybody in the White House, all the ones who stay
loyal, because the president has unlimited presidential
pardon power. PPP! And doesn't that mean the
president could even pardon the president? PPP!
It's probably never been done, but that's what Trump
does—what's never been done before!*

*NUMBER FOUR: In 2018 the immigration guys will
unfortunately have to deport Melania. It will be
tragic. So tragic. But I can't make an exception!
She's an illegal! I didn't realize at the time! So sad as
she returns home to Yugoslavia, sad, the Aeroflot 747
taking off from Andrews, on all the TV channels, so
sad, me and Barron waving bye-bye, maybe I even
cry, one tear, close-up, bye-bye. My poll numbers
go crazy.*

*NUMBER FIVE: Speaking of too bad, I won't be able
to pardon Jared because he's related to me, and that
would be completely illegal. But if Ivanka divorces
him, then I could pardon him. And then she and I,
we'd both be divorced, we'd have that in common,
too—the two smartest, blondest, most amazing people
in America, maybe in the world, both Trumps,
suddenly single. Such a powerful idea. I have
goose bumps right now thinking about it.*

*MITZI: Book a table at Majorelle, nice cozy corner
table, tomorrow at 8 p.m., Vanksy and me, tell Secret
Service.*

*NUMBER FIVE: In 2018 Rodrigo definitely becomes
secretary of state, for the first time a somewhat*

foreign secretary of state, plus he's a minority, so people will love that, hooray President Trump, hooray Presidente Trump, hooray President Trump in Russian with the crazy backward 3 in it, hooray!

NUMBER FIVE: In my second term, when I can start doing whatever I want and my son is old enough to become White House chief of staff, we'll build the bridge I had him design, the longest in the world, Alaska to Russia, fifty-five miles according to Barron, so much better than NAFTA and so much stronger than the EU, partners again, this time in the war on terror, all our nuclear combined, the first double-super-duper power. Did you know if you scramble the letters in "USA, Sir!" it makes "Russia!"? Amazing, right? I think that's actually in the Bible.

I know Congress and the Pentagon and "intelligence" and crooked Hillary and sick Obama will fight me on the bridge and the rest of it, like they did against Fredric March in *Seven Days in May*, like they killed Kennedy. In fact, they could be sending in a secret SWAT team right now to take me out.

"Anthony?"

Anthony didn't answer. I really should have my own gun. I opened one of the blanket doors on the fort. They muffle everything.

"*Anthony?*"

"Everything okay in there, Mr. President? Ready to go down for dinner?"

"A-OK, Anthony, Mogul is outstanding, better than ever, skipping dinner tonight, watching the pounds, working on the book, et cetera, just wanted to make sure you're out there, ha ha ha, in case of enemy things. Thanks."

What number was I on in my 2018 plan? Whatever.

> *MITZI:*
> *Make the numbers all go in order. Thanks, Mitzi. You are the best.*

★ ★ ★ ★ ★ ★ ★ ★

THE END

A ll the Diet Coke, all the vitamins and supplements, didn't sleep a week, didn't slip a wink, no sleep slink last Thursday, people die in their sleep, if I sleep then they get me, the resistance, the terrorists, ISIS, Obama and Hillary created ISIS, it's true, so true, so evil.

I was fooled bad by Anthony, but now I realize who Anthony is— that famous secret black son of Bill Clinton from the Internet, Hillary and Obama put him in the Secret Service, the *Secret* Service, *that's* collusion, *he's* the wiretapper, him and his buddy Robert Pattinson, I get it, so illegal, so evil.

I could walk out there, I say hey Anthony, beautiful new MP-5 we got you, dozen rounds a second on full auto, cool, can I hold it, take a photo, Fifth Avenue in the background, you lookin' at me? you lookin' at me? are you angry? *buh-buh-buh-buh-buh*, you're not resistance, *I'm* resistance, *buh-buh-buh-buh-buh*, I'm commando in chief!

Oh my God! Incredible! Amazing! *So much coverage*, the most coverage of anything ever in history! And it *wasn't* the president's fault! That dead black agent who looked so much like Obama, Clinton's son, that's what people say, why did he hand the president his weapon, maybe trying to frame him, so tragic, how terrible for the president, we still believe in him, we still trust him, we love Trump so much. Ivanka agrees, like Cosby's grown-up daughter Rudy Huxtable at his trial, believed in her dad, stood by her man.

My mother predicted all of this. "A colored man with a gun," she said many, many times.

They'd need *twenty* Republicans in the Senate to convict me of anything, no way they get that, maybe ten, twelve tops, but even if they put me on trial in a real court I *still* get off, like Cosby and OJ and Baretta and all celebrities, no-lose, totally no-lose, not guilty, greatest reality show ever, monster ratings, vindicated, win-win-win-win-win-win, The End.

Sunrise! Feeling *fantastic*! *Amazing* energy! TGIF!

5-4-3-2-1. 5-4-3-2-1. Always the same. 5-4-3-2-1.

Here's what's going to happen now. We evacuate New York on my command. Because no one knows exactly what's going to happen now.

The dogs need to be captured and shaved, all of them, so they can be properly identified, and then sent back, all of them.

And every woman has to get down on the ground, lie down, to be ready. Protection.

I want Barron out of the country in one of the top-secret places. Now. Because it's showtime. I'm pretty sure it's showtime.

"Hey, Anthony? You awake out there? Because the president has got a question."

ACKNOWLEDGMENTS

We gratefully acknowledge Lorne Michaels and the cast and crew of *Saturday Night Live*, particularly Chris Kelly and Sarah Schneider, who have written many of *SNL*'s Donald Trump sketches, and who contributed ideas for the photographs in *You Can't Spell America Without Me*. Thanks also to Steve Higgins. Louis Zakarian, Jodi Mancuso, and Michael Anzalone create the hair, makeup, and wardrobe design, respectively, for Alec's *SNL* appearances as Trump—work that Jodi and Michael did for the photo shoots here as well.

Our collaborators at Penguin Press have been nothing but supportive and enthusiastic—especially Scott Moyers, Ann Godoff, Claire Vaccaro, Darren Hagger, Christopher Richards, Kiara Barrow, Matt Boyd, and Sarah Hutson.

Thanks to creative director Bonnie Siegler at Eight and a Half, and designers Adam Lehman, Kellie Pcolar, and Kristen Ren.

We're grateful to our photographer Mark Seliger, as well as production coordinator Coco Knudson.

Thanks also to Mary Ellen Matthews for additional photography, to location scout Ernie Liberati, production designer Rob Strauss, location coordinator Lu-Ann Russell, makeup artist Jason Milani, and photo retouchers Rachel Crowe and Salvatore Fibbri. And to our actors Shea Glasser (as the Trump women), Derek Brantley (as the Secret Service agent), and Earl Gatachalian (as the White House steward). We are especially grateful to Jim Warlick, whose Presidential Experience supplied our Oval Office, and to his colleague Alesia Jones. Thanks, Milton Glaser, for lending us your Trump-brand vodka, and David Owen, for explaining golf.

Alec wishes to thank Karen Gantz. And, especially, his wife, Hilaria, for soldiering through an *SNL* season of Trump and all that went with that.

Kurt thanks Suzanne Gluck, Eric Zohn, and Alicia Glekas Everett at WME, as well as George Sheanshang and Eric Rayman. And he's grateful to Anne Kreamer for enduring the months of Trump-channeling and for being his first reader.

ABOUT THE AUTHORS

Alec Baldwin has performed on stage and television and in more than sixty films. His work has earned him an Oscar nomination (for *The Cooler*), a Tony nomination, two Emmy awards, three Golden Globes, and seven consecutive SAG Awards for *30 Rock*. He holds a BFA in drama and an honorary doctorate from NYU-Tisch. The Hilaria and Alec Baldwin Foundation supports many organizations and causes in the arts and public policy. He is also the author of *A Promise to Ourselves* and a memoir, *Nevertheless*. He is married to Hilaria Thomas Baldwin and has four children: Ireland, Carmen, Rafael, and Leonardo.

★ ★

Kurt Andersen is the *New York Times* bestselling author of three critically acclaimed novels, most recently *True Believers*. His non-fiction books include *Fantasyland*, *Reset*, and *The Real Thing*. He has also written for TV, film, and the theater. In addition, he's host and co-creator of *Studio 360*, the Peabody Award–winning public radio program, and a regular contributor to *The New York Times* and *Vanity Fair*. Previously, he was a columnist and critic for *The New Yorker* and *Time*, served as editor in chief of *New York*, and co-founded *Spy* magazine.